Mysteries and Miracles
of California

By Jack Kutz

Rhombus Publishing Company

Cover design and illustrations
by Mary Robert

Rhombus Publishing Company, Inc.
P.O. Box 806, Corrales, New Mexico 87048

Contents

Foreword

Any way you look at it, California blows your mind. From the madness of its freeways to the solitude of its desert wilderness, from the glamour of Hollywood to the unpretentious rusticity of the small towns and the majesty of it seacoasts and mountains, California offers more variety than any other state in the Union.

When one thinks of California, images of Disneyland, Yosemite, movie studios, and San Francisco cable cars come immediately to mind. But the state is fantastic in other, much less publicized ways as well. There is an aura of mystery that also hangs over the state, subtle but very real and ever present.

California is haunted. The per capita number of ghosts is definitely above the national average. But California's spooks are far from the ordinary, garden variety of spirits. Many California ghosts are famous movie stars and multi-millionaires.

In California, if one life is not enough, all you

have to do is live a second one. Belief in reincarnation runs strong and many actors and actresses have, to their own satisfaction, proven they have lived previous lives.

More UFOs have been sighted in California's skies than almost anywhere else and California holds the world's record for the number of close encounters of the third kind. More Californians claim to have ridden in flying saucers than astronauts have gone into outer space.

And what of the scores of tales of lost treasures? If only half of them are really true, California is indeed America's Golden State.

California's mysteries are both contemporary and ancient. From a time when Indians ate fire and built inscrutable monuments in the desert to the seances and age regression hypnotic sessions of today, California has always been in the forefront of the arcane. Yet her mysteries go mostly unnoticed.

References to these strange tales are scattered and few and far between. Never before have California's mysteries been brought together in a single volume. This is the first attempt to gather as many mysteries as possible into one brief book. Still, this is more than just a collection of bizarre stories. It is also meant as a guidebook. Whenever possible, I have included directions for visiting these special places since a surprising number of them are open to the general public.

Nonetheless, most visitors to these enchanted localities are unaware of the fascinating stories behind them. They have no way of knowing that the hotel where they stayed has a phantom lurking on the third floor, or that the ghost town they toured actually is populated by the ghosts of its former residents, or that the desert wildlands they drove through are full of captivating wonders if only they had known where to look.

Most of California's esoteric phenomena are ongoing; they repeat themselves over and over again so that if one is lucky enough to be at the right place at the right time, one can personally experience the unbelievable.

On the other hand, many of California's mysterious happenings are completely unexpected and no guidebook can tell where and when they will occur. For example, no one can predict the appearance of a UFO though the chances of seeing one in California are greater than nearly anywhere else.

So, marvel at the facts contained in this book, visit the mysterious sites if you wish and enjoy the other side of the Golden State of California.

1

Enigmas of the California Deserts

Where on this earth is there a better place to search for mysteries than the desert? Is there anywhere else on this small but diverse planet where so many mystic wonders can be found? The deserts of the world seem to hold more secrets and inexplicable riddles than any other earthly realm. This is certainly true of the California deserts.

From the windswept Colorado Desert to the mighty Mohave and on north to the pulsing heat waves of Death Valley, a harsh, beautiful, and mysterious landscape sprawls out across more than 300 miles of crescent dunes, ancient volcanoes, and dry brackish seas. Scorching Santa Ana winds howl like banshees through the bone-dry basins. Forests of shaggy Joshua trees stand like legions of lost souls with their arms raised warning trespassers to go

1

away. Billowing smoke trees waver like diaphanous ghosts in the sandy washes.

In these great wastelands, many unbelievable discoveries have been made and desert wanderers never know what they may chance upon as they roam. One such wanderer was a young mule driver traveling with the famous Spanish explorer Juan Bautista de Anza whose expedition crossed the southern California desert in 1775.

De Anza rolled his caravan over the unmapped wilderness with the absolute certainty that he was the first European ever to see these lands. Somewhere west of the Colorado river, he sent the muleteer out ahead of the others to search for water.

The young fellow rode alone past a long, low, barren mountain range until he reached a wide dune field spreading out toward the horizon like an immobile ocean. He led his mule to the crest of the highest dune, from which he could see many miles. His eyes searched the lifeless waves of sand in hope of spying some sign of an oasis but there was nothing. He was about to turn away and move on when he caught sight of something in the distance that stopped him in his tracks.

Surely, the lonely muleteer must have thought the heat was causing him to hallucinate for what he was seeing could not possibly be real. There, half buried in the sand 100 miles from the nearest waterway, sat a great Spanish galleon.

"*Un espejismo*," the awed man mumbled. "A mirage. It will vanish when I approach it." He rode closer but the ship did not disappear. In less than an hour, he was standing in its shadow.

The vessel was clearly very old. Its sails had rotted and fallen; the riggings crumbled in the mule driver's hands when he clutched them. Cautiously, he climbed on board and stepped across the creaking, sun-bleached planks of the deck. The doorway to the hold had blown open long ago and the interior was nearly filled with sand. In one corner, however, the top of a medium-sized oaken chest was visible.

The muleteer dragged the chest up onto the deck, broke it open and let out a joyous laugh. Inside were six plump, canvas pouches full of luxurious, milky-white pearls. He wasted no time in stuffing the pouches into the mule's pack, and promptly became the first and only man to desert from De Anza's expedition. He headed west by himself until he reached the little mission settlement of San Diego on the coast of Alta California.

When he told the surprised padres about his incredible discovery, they quickly informed him it was his sacred duty to give the pearls to the church. The mule driver refused to do so. He left the mission and was never seen again.

During the next hundred years, several other desert travelers claimed to have seen the same ship. It was gradually decaying; the masts had toppled and the hull had caved in. Apparently, it eventually disintegrated completely for no further sightings were reported after the middle of the nineteenth century.

The whole unbelievable story would probably have been dismissed as just another desert myth were it not for the research of an early California historian, Florence Haines Apponyi. In 1885, she discovered archival proof that a Spanish galleon actually did sail into the California desert.

Apponyi had been leafing through some very old, long-neglected early Spanish historical documents when she chanced upon the journal of an obscure sea captain named Juan de Iturbe. In the year of 1615, Iturbe and his stalwart crew had sailed along the coast of the Gulf of California diving for pearls.

Their venture had been a very rewarding one. Now, they were ready to return to Spain. In those days when so little was known about the American continent, it was rumored that there was a great waterway called the Strait of Anian which ran all the way from the Gulf of California to the Gulf of Mexico. Iturbe decided to search for this fabled passageway and take a shortcut home.

He sailed to the upper end of the Gulf, where, to his delight, he found a navigable channel extending inland between two mountain ranges. Iturbe followed the strait until he reached a giant lake covering the area known today as the Cahuilla Basin. He circled the lake seeking the continuation of the channel, but, in a matter of days, realized he had come to a dead end.

The "lake" was a catch-basin into which the Colorado River poured its floodwaters at periodic intervals. The waterway Iturbe had sailed in on was an outflow channel which carried excess waters south to the gulf when the lake reached a high enough level to overflow the silt dike on the coastline.

In dismay, the Spanish captain realized that the lake was draining rapidly. He hurriedly sailed back to the outlet but he was too late. The once-wide channel was down to a trickle and sandbars blocked the way. Juan de Iturbe's proud galleon was landlocked. He and his crew had no choice but to abandon the ship and trudge off to Mexico.

It is not hard to believe that Iturbe's lake did once exist. From time to time throughout history, the Colorado's flood waters have created some sizeable desert lakes. The latest and largest was the Salton Sea, which was formed in 1905 when the Colorado River overflowed.

So, the legend of the lost Spanish galleon may well be a true and acceptable story. But, there is a second tale about a second desert ship which is much stranger and far more difficult to explain. This mysterious craft was discovered in 1873 by a desert traveler named Santiago Socia.

At the time, Socia was running from the law for having killed a man in a saloon fight in Los Angeles. The fugitive had ridden rapidly southeast away from the populated coastal areas and into the hot, dry, uninhabited wastelands, seeking a remote route to Mexico and safety. He had almost reached the border when he came upon the ship.

Socia reined in his weary horse and gaped open mouthed at this astounding sight. The ancient vessel was silhouetted against a tall canyon wall, poised on the sand as if ready to sail away across the dunes. Not only was the ship obviously out of place, but it was definitely not a Spanish ship. Unlike the bulky, sea-plowing galleons of Spain, this boat was narrow, sleek, and elegant. Its long, curved bow was as graceful as the neck of a swan, and, on its sides, a series of shield-shaped metal discs had been mounted.

Santiago Socia stared at the ship for several long minutes. Then, after vowing to return someday to explore the sand-filled hull, he rode on to Mexicali. Soon his wife, Petra, joined him, and they became subsistence farmers on a small plot of land outside of town.

As he tilled the fields, Santiago often thought about the strange ship. Could there be a treasure on board? he wondered. Finally, he returned to the desert and found the vessel, but, though he dug out all the sand, he found nothing of value. Socia pried off a wagon load of boards and tossed one of the metal discs on top of them. He used the boards to build a sturdy hog pen on his farm; the disc he gave to Petra, who used it for many years as a *comal* upon which she fried tortillas.

A number of the Socias' friends also went to see the ship and to help themselves to the free hardwood lumber. When a prospector named Jim Tucker visited the site just after the turn of the century, he reported that the fabled craft was now in pretty sorry shape. The once-proud seabird was starting to look like a turkey carcass on the day after Thanksgiving.

In all probability, the desert buried the ship's bones for it has not been seen in recent times. There is no longer any physical evidence that it ever existed, and, until 1922, no one could even theorize about where the ship might have come from. One night during that year, Julian Lander, an anthropologist who was doing studies of the Seri Indians on Tiburon Island in the Gulf of California, was listening to the Indians sing their traditional songs.

The Seri, who have lived on the coastlands and islands of the gulf for uncounted centuries, have always preserved their history in songs and stories. One song in particular fascinated Lander more than any other. His interpreter, who spoke both Seri and Spanish, told him the ballad's title was "Came From Afar Men."

As the Seri elders sang and strummed their one-string fiddles, the interpreter translated the story: Once, long ago, a beautiful bird-like vessel came floating up the coastline. The "bird's" great, white wings were spread out above its dark body. Its long neck was raised high above the water. When the bird reached the Seri village, it stopped and folded its wings.

Several men and one woman left the floating bird and came ashore. Each of the men had hair as golden as the sun; the woman's hair was as red as fire and all of them had eyes that were bluer than seawater. The woman and one of the men waited in the village while the others went inland to hunt deer with bows and arrows. When they returned with their game, they all climbed back onto the bird. It spread its wings again, swam north, and never came back.

Lander was spellbound by the tale. To him, the bird sounded much like a Viking ship but common sense told him it could not have been. He knew that there was a growing belief that the Norsemen had crossed the Atlantic well ahead of Columbus, but, in 1922, this was far from conclusive. It would not be until 1930 that Viking relics would be found in Ontario and even more years would pass before the ruins of the Norse settlements in New England would be uncovered.

Eventually, a great wealth of Viking artifacts surfaced across much of the United States... spearheads in Wisconsin, runestones in Oklahoma, a petroglyph of a sea serpent-like ship's figurehead in New Mexico, and a depiction of a man in a horned helmet wielding a battle axe in Colorado. Taken altogether, this sizeable collection of Nordic memorabilia proves beyond doubt that the bold Vikings once toured the eastern seaboard, followed the coastline of the Gulf of Mexico, sailed up the Mississippi, the Arkansas and Rio Grande rivers, and explored the lands on both sides of the rivers.

The Vikings traveled extensively between A.D.

1000 and A.D. 1350, but it seems almost inconceivable that they could have made a voyage all the way to California. To do so would have meant sailing around the entire southern hemisphere of the New World.

If a Viking ship actually did succeed in making such a journey, it was a magnificent achievement. How ironic it is that after such a monumental odyssey, the ill-fated ship was lured by the desert into a trap –a shallow, disappearing lake from which there was no escape.

Deserts are always full of surprises; here one should expect the unexpected. In fact, in the desert even the rocks cannot be trusted to behave the way they should.

In the northwestern corner of Death Valley National Monument lies a hidden valley known as Racetrack Playa. It is a small valley just two miles wide and three miles long —a waterless lake as flat as a pool table, drier than beef jerky, and bleak as a moonscape. Racetrack Playa's featureless surface is cracked into a gray mosaic of sun-baked clay cobblestones surrounded by formidable mountain guardians.

Here and there, rocks from those mountains rest on the floor of this dead mud flat, poised like chess pieces waiting to be moved by the hands of Mother Nature. And every so often, like all chess pieces, the rocks do move. They slide forward, crushing the parched soil into powder as they scoot along. Usually, they travel in straight lines but some of them have been known to veer off at right angles and a few have made complete loops.

The tracks vary in length from ten feet to over 200, although once an 800-foot furrow was observed and measured. The limestone boulders differ greatly in size; many are no bigger than softballs while others are estimated to weigh between 200 and 600 pounds. No one has actually seen the rocks in motion but neither has anyone ever doubted that they have actually moved.

The first reports of this remarkable phenomenon were made by prospectors in the early 1900s but no scientific studies were done until the 1950s. This early research resulted in considerable debate and disagreement over the causes of the rocks' movements but several theories were cautiously advanced.

Some geologists thought it possible that highly magnetic mineral deposits below ground might be drawing the stones slowly but inexorably across the surface. Others wondered if the gravitational pull of the moon was somehow tugging at the rocks or perhaps sunspots were in some way responsible.

None of these theories seemed very plausible. It appeared much more likely that wind was the force moving the rocks. But even that explanation didn't gain much acceptance until, in the 1960s, laboratory experiments showed that a wind of 100 miles per hour or more was capable of moving objects the size of the Racetrack boulders, though only under a precise combination of weather conditions.

The Playa would have to be wet and slippery. The depth of the moisture would have to be three to four centimeters but no more than that, since deeper mud would sink the rocks just enough to greatly increase the force needed to push them forward. If ice was also present, "ice collars" would form around the rocks and allow them to go skating. Is this then the solution to the mystery? Until a better explanation is offered it will have to do.

Stranger things than rocks have moved across the desolate floors of the California deserts. In January of 1964, Victor Stoyanow, a former U.S. Marine Corps Major whose retirement hobby was searching for lost mines, ran across a trail of footprints in a very remote part of the lower Borrego Valley. The footprints were so weird they made the hair stand up on the back of his neck.

On a brisk winter morning, Stoyanow had driven beyond Carrizo Creek toward the base of the Superstition Hills to a tiny waterhole known as Harper's Well. He parked his Jeep beneath the tamarisks that surround this meager source of water and hiked up to the top of a nearby promontory to orient his location with a compass.

After he had gotten his bearings, he walked back downhill by a slightly different route. At the base of the sandy knoll, Stoyanow came upon two parallel lines of footprints heading off toward the distant hills. Puzzled, he knelt to examine them.

The tracks had obviously been made by bare feet but they were oddly shaped. The heel prints were about three inches across while the pads above the instep were over six inches wide. Each print was eight inches long, had five blunt toes, and had been pressed into the sand at 40-inch intervals.

Stoyanow judged them to be about two days old since the impressions had clearly been made after a heavy rain soaked the desert during the previous week. The trackmakers had shambled along side by side most of their way, but, as Stoyanow followed them, he noticed they occasionally moved a few yards apart as they passed around boulders or bushes.

Within a quarter of a mile, the footprints abruptly halted at the base of an upwardly swooping sand dune. Stoyanow looked around in every direction but the tracks went no farther. He scrambled awkwardly up the rippled slope to the crest of the dune, where to his amazement, both sets of footprints reappeared just beyond the rim, their heels driven deep into the soft sand.

The utterly perplexed old major glanced back down. The distance between the lower tracks and the upper ones was a good 20 feet and the rise in elevation was at least ten. Could the creatures have possibly leaped that high and that far?

The footprints continued to head on toward the hills but Stoyanow hesitated to follow them any farther. He was getting more than a little nervous. With squinted eyes, he carefully scanned the empty landscape for any sign of movement. But the desert was motionless as a freeze-frame and so silent it seemed to be holding its breath. Stoyanow was alone in the middle of nowhere, and, though he could see nothing to be afraid of, he felt a sense of dread. He hurried back to his Jeep and drove away.

During the days that followed, Stoyanow continued to wonder what in the world he had stumbled onto. By the weekend, his curiosity was greater than his fear so he returned to Harper's Well. This time, he was accompanied by two friends, a big game hunter named Robert Speccy and an archeology student, Bob Wilson. As the Jeep bounced along the rutted road, Wilson speculated as to what the creatures might be. "Bears, maybe?", he asked.

"Ain't no bears out in that desert, Bob," the hunter said. Stoyanow agreed and added, "Even if there were, they would have had to have been walking on their hind legs."

When Victor Stoyanow brought his Jeep to a

stop at the edge of the waterhole, the three men stared in astonishment at the scene around them. The area near the tamarisk grove was now criss-crossed by scores of footprints identical to the origi-nal ones. The creatures had followed Stoyanow's tracks and, when they reached the oasis, they seemed to have gone into a rage. In places, Stoyanow's foot-prints had been furiously clawed out by paws or hands that had scattered the sand about as if in a wild fit of pique.

At the spot where Stoyanow had parked before, the lower branches of a tree had been torn off and thrown on his tire tracks. Speccy studied them with his hands on his hips. "Victor," he drawled, "I don't believe them branches're meant to be a welcome mat. I think whatever the hell done this is tryin' to send you a message."

"And I read that message loud and clear," the old soldier said. "May I suggest we make an orderly but hasty strategic withdrawal? Or, as the enlisted men used to say, 'Let's bug out!'" The three unnerved men quickly abandoned their plans for an overnight camp out, hopped back in their Jeep, and bumped off down the trail to civilization.

Stoyanow was never to know what kind of rowdy beasts he had disturbed in that forlorn desert cirque. The drifting winds soon erased the tracks, brushing them away and smoothing out the sand as if they had never been there.

Many desert mysteries, however, have left per-manent imprints on the land and although they can-not be completely explained, they remain ever pre-sent, waiting for anyone willing to search them out. The Sleeping Giants of Blythe are good examples.

These mysterious wonders, like so many other

curious aberrations, were discovered quite accidentally by a lone desert traveler. This time, however, the
traveler was not tramping around the desert on foot;
he was flying above it.

George A. Palmer was a former World War I pilot
who operated a small general aviation airport in Las
Vegas, Nevada in the 1930s. One day in 1931, he flew
to Blythe to visit his brother. While passing over the
flat, stony terrain east of the Maria Mountains, he was
startled to see the huge white figure of a spread-
eagled man carved in the dark volcanic rubble below
him.

Palmer brought his plane down to 2,000 feet and
circled above the figure. He widened his circle and
soon spotted a second, equally impressive giant along
with a four-legged animal with a long tail. The excited
aviator flew on to Blythe, where, upon landing, he
asked the local citizens about the figures. No one had
ever heard of them.

In the morning, Palmer invited a local photographer, Charles E. Barrows, to fly with him over the site.
"I don't believe what I'm seein'," Barrows repeated
over and over as he clicked his camera. Once Palmer
got back to Las Vegas, he sent copies of Barrow's photos to the Los Angeles Museum in Exhibition Park.

The museum's curator of anthropology, Arthur
Woodward, immediately sent Palmer a letter. "Mr.
Palmer," he wrote, "You have made a real discovery.
So far as I know, figures of this kind have never before
been reported. I would very much like to go out and
study them on the ground."

"There is no better time to do that than right
now," Palmer wrote back. "The desert is cool this
time of year. Meet me in Blythe as soon as you can."

Two weeks later, Woodward, along with archeologist Charles Van Bergen, arrived in the tiny desert town. Palmer was waiting for them so they all drove at once to the desolate piece of land that no one else had bothered to visit. Following Palmer, the professors walked across the coarse basalt gravel directly to the sprawled-out giants, then over to the long-legged animal. Near this quadruped, they also discovered a depiction of a coiled snake.

"What do you make of all this, Dr. Woodward?" Palmer asked.

"These are what we call intaglios," Woodward replied. "They differ from petroglyphs which were pecked onto rocks and pictographs which were painted on because intaglios were made by scraping away the surface of the ground." He squatted on his haunches and picked up a stone. "See how the upper side of this rock is blackened by its exposure to the elements? Look at the other side —it's gray, almost white.

"When the dark stones have been pushed aside, a lighter layer of rock is revealed. These are *very* impressive intaglios. I've *never* seen any this large." He got out his tape measure. "Let's see just how big they really are."

The longest figure turned out to be 167 feet from head to toe, and the second was exactly 95 feet long. The nimble-footed beast was close to 58 feet from nose to rump and the serpentine coil was 11 by 17 feet.

"Who could have made these?" Palmer wondered. "And when? And why?"

Arthur Woodward laughed. "George, during the next few years, you're going to hear dozens of answers to those questions. And there's a good possibility that none of the explanations will even

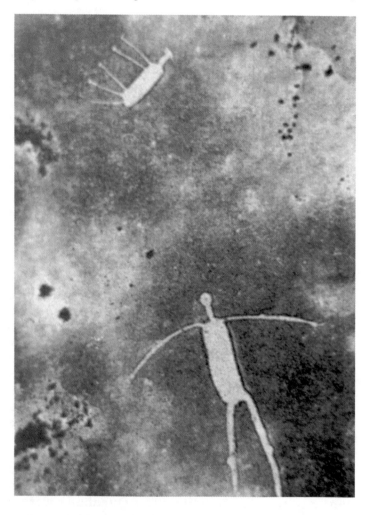

THE GIANT INTAGLIOS. Are the drawings in the desert near Blythe mystical dreams or ominous guardians?

Desert Magazine Archives

come close to the truth."

The old anthropologist was certainly right about the controversy; to this day, people still argue over the origins and meanings of the Blythe intaglios.

The first hypothesis was that the figures were created to pay homage to a legendary Pima warrior who killed a dreadful monster which was terrorizing the tribe. This theory was quickly dismissed because the Pima live some 200 miles east of the site.

Many people believed that the four-legged animal provided the best clue for solving the mystery. At first, it was assumed the creature was a horse. If so, that would mean that the spectacular artwork was done after the Spanish arrival but others pointed out that the animal's long, skinny tail did not in any way resemble a horse's tail. It looked much more like the tail of a cougar.

This has led some to speculate that the intaglios might be Mohave Indian creations, since one of the Mohave's myths tells of a wondrous supernatural cougar which has the power to bestow great hunting skills on any man who chances to dream of it. Perhaps, the Sleeping Giants are dreaming of that magical cougar. When viewed from above, the mighty animal does seem to be drifting toward the slumbering figures. Yet there is another possible explanation. Anthropologists have determined that the land beyond the site was once the domain of the Quechan Indians. These nomads' ancient realm extended all the way from the Gila River to the present-day town of Needles. The Quechans were a fierce and aggressive people who tolerated no intruders on their lands. According to the diaries of the Spanish friars who tried in vain to convert them to Catholicism, they were strong and very tall, well over six feet. And, interestingly, they kept dogs.

When one compares the size of the animal intaglio to the much larger human figures, it does seem proportionate to a medium-sized dog. Further, the coiled intaglios may not necessarily be snakes as originally assumed.

The Quechan symbol for water was a spiraled circle representing a spring. The literal translation of the word Quechan is "he who wades in water." The neighboring tribes referred to the Quechan as the "water people", probably because they controlled and jealously guarded all streams and waterholes in their vast, arid lands.

It may be that the intaglios were meant to be very large "No Trespassing" signs. Two tall human figures accompanied by a mean-looking watchdog and a Quechan water symbol can easily be construed as a firm warning to stay out of Quechan country.

Whether the Sleeping Giants are territorial markers, commemorations of primordial creation myths or something else altogether cannot be decisively proven. But then, no one can prove or disprove that strange creatures prowl around Harper's Well or that the winds play chess with enormous boulders on Racetrack Playa. Nor can anyone convincingly argue that the remnants of great sailing ships do or do not lie beneath the desert's sands.

Apparently, that's the way the desert wants it to be. It always seems to reveal just enough of its many secrets to puzzle the discoverers but rarely enough to allow them to completely solve the mysteries. The desert likes to keep its visitors guessing.

How to Visit the Floating Boulders & Sleeping Giant Intaglios

To reach Racetrack Playa, drive northwest from the Death Valley National Monument visitor's center for 55 miles to the turnoff to Ubehebe Crater. From the crater, head south on an improved but washboard road 17 miles to Teakettle Junction. The right fork takes you on to the Racetrack. Vehicles are prohibited on the playa surface but it's all right to get out and walk.

The Sleeping Giant intaglios can be reached by traveling 17 miles north from Blythe on U.S. Highway 95 to a turnoff on a gravel road. A parking place is located half a mile from the turnoff. The fenced figures can then be approached on foot.

Bibliography - Chapter 1

Barette, Keith. *Desert Magazine.* Palm Desert, California. August, 1979.

Corliss, William R. **Handbook of Unusual Natural Phenomena**. New York. Arlington House, Inc. 1986.

Fell, Barry. **Saga America**. New York. Times Books. 1980.

Jaeger, Edmund C. **The California Deserts.** Stanford, California. Stanford University Press. 1965.

Pepper, Choral. *Desert Magazine.* Palm Desert, California. October, 1966. November, 1980. June, 1981.

Stoyanow, Victor. *Desert Magazine.* Palm Desert, California. July, 1964.

2

Mrs. Winchester's
Macabre Mansion

Fear can be one of life's greatest motivators. The constant need to protect one's self from life's many threats and perils compels almost everyone to go to lengths to ensure their personal safety. Deadbolts on doors, smoke detectors on ceilings and emergency numbers by the telephone give a measure of assurance that one's home is safe.

However, when the fear of bodily harm comes from a supernatural source, when the danger is something that cannot be locked out or driven away, frightened people often resort to desperate and seemingly irrational ways of protecting themselves. It was this sort of extreme paranoia that led to the creation of California's weirdest dwelling: "The Winchester Mystery House" of San Jose.

Called grotesque by some and an architectural

masterpiece by others, Sarah Pardee Winchester's sprawling 160-room mansion stands today as a memorial to one woman's obsessive fear of the super-natural.

Sarah Pardee was born in 1839 in New Haven, Connecticut. She grew up to become a very pretty but tiny young lady. Sarah stood only four feet, ten inch-es tall and weighed a mere 100 pounds. As the daughter of an upper class New Haven family, she enjoyed all the advantages and privileges that the local gentry bestowed upon themselves. Sarah Pardee was highly educated, fluent in four languages, and an accomplished pianist. Her charm and grace always made her the "belle of the ball" at New Haven's lavish social events.

At the age of 23, she was courted by William Wirt Winchester, the son of the inventor and manufac-turer of the "gun that won the West" —the Winchester repeating rifle. The young, diminutive woman and her tall, handsome suitor must have made a stunning couple as they swirled around the dance floor beneath the glittering chandeliers.

Sarah and William married in 1862. Two years later, Sarah Winchester gave birth to a baby girl but the child died within a few weeks. For Sarah, it was an almost unbearable loss. Soon afterward, William also died suddenly. Now, Sarah was totally devastat-ed. In her grief, she became very reclusive, shunning friends and relatives alike. On the rare occasions she went out in public, she was always heavily veiled.

The young widow's closest friends grew very worried, and, whenever Sarah permitted them to visit her, the things she told them only increased their anxiety. Sarah said she was being tormented by dreadful spirits which came at night to tell her they

THE WINCHESTER MANSION. Forever haunted, its tower bell was rung nightly to summon spirits to the Blue Séance Room.

True West Magazine

planned to kill her as they had killed her husband and daughter.

This wild talk greatly alarmed Sarah's friends. They tried to convince her that she was not in danger, that she was only having nightmares, but Sarah swore the ghosts were real. She gradually became so terrified that she sought advice from a spiritualist in Boston.

Sarah Winchester told no one except her trusted carriage driver, Charles Farnham, where she was going or why. She directed Farnham to take her to one of Boston's oldest, shabbiest neighborhoods and ordered him to halt her elegant brougham buggy in front of an aged, dilapidated house.

A light rain was falling so Farnham raised an umbrella over Sarah as he escorted her to the door. He twisted the brass doorbell key several times before the door creaked open and a sharp-faced, black-haired woman in a long, dark shawl peered out.

"Are you Mrs. Raven?" Sarah asked from behind her veil.

"I am," the expressionless woman answered. "Please come in. I've been expecting you." She made a dismissive hand movement at Sarah's chauffeur; Farnham tapped the shiny visor of his cap and walked back to the carriage where he sat uncomfortably and apprehensively for the next two hours.

It was almost completely dark when Sarah emerged from the unlighted house. "Take me home," was all she said as her driver opened the carriage door for her. She drew her brocaded lap robe around her and rode in silence for many miles before she spoke again. Leaning forward, she said, "Farnham, I am more frightened now than I have ever been.

"Mrs. Raven held a séance in her parlor. The

spirits came and spoke through her. They are very evil spirits who have put a curse on the Winchester family and have sworn to avenge the thousands of people killed by the Winchester rifle. Mrs. Raven says my only chance of survival is to go as far away as I can and build a house within which the spirits will never find me.

"She also said there are good spirits near me. They will try to protect me and guide me to a place where I will be safe. Farnham, I must leave Connecticut as soon as possible."

Less than a week later, the distraught Sarah told all her friends, relatives, and servants that she would be moving away. She did not reveal her destination but said it would be "far, far from New England." Only her niece, Margaret Merriam, and the faithful Farnham volunteered to go with her. No doubt, they were both worried about her mental stability.

Sometime in 1884, the three of them arrived in San Jose, California. Beyond the outskirts of town, Sarah found a rather grand 18-room farmhouse standing on an open plain. "This is the place," she stated assuredly. "Mrs. Raven said that when I saw it, I would know. She was right."

Sarah bought the house at once, had it completely renovated and began adding on additional rooms. As Sarah had inherited over $20 million dollars from William Winchester, money was no object. In a day and age when a newspaper cost two pennies and a restaurant meal could be had for a quarter, Sarah spent an average of $2,000 a week on the construction of her ever-expanding mansion.

Over a period of 37 years, she spent $5.5 million on the monumental project that was never entirely finished, and was never intended to be. As the years passed, the original house grew into an ever-spreading compound encompassing 40 bedrooms, nine kitchens, 13 bathrooms, 40 staircases, 47 fireplaces, and 52 skylights. Towers and conical turrets rose in profusion above the balconies and porches that surrounded each section of the interconnected subdivision which Sarah named *Llanada Villa* —the House on the Plain.

Llanada Villa has over 10,000 windows, most of which are made of exquisite Belgian stained glass. Each window's casement latch is patterned after the bolt of the Winchester rifle and is unlocked by pulling a trigger. The highly polished floors of the vast mansion are all either hand-laid, imported hardwood, or geometrically arranged European tiles. Some of the bedroom floors are designed to change colors as the light passes over them during the day.

Sarah Winchester's sumptuous extravagance created an architectural marvel, but *Llanada Villa* is more than just a tribute to one woman's flamboyance. It was designed to be a maze —a confusing labyrinth through which no evil spirits could possibly find their way. Throughout the mansion, there are hallways and corridors that lead nowhere. Many tall, wide doors open onto blank walls and several stairways rise up and end at the ceiling. In some rooms, cabinet doors can be swung out to reveal shelves a mere one inch deep. Many of the fireplace chimneys are bricked in, and the skylights are often in the floor.

A number of rooms were lavishly furnished and decorated before being completely sealed off, never to be opened again during Sarah's lifetime.

Outside the mansion's walls, the expensive, well manicured grounds are equally bewildering and protective. Hedged pathways wander off to dead ends or thick barricades of bushes backed by barbed wire. In one of the bowers, a bronze statue of an Indian warrior stands with his bow and arrow poised to defend *Llanada Villa* from intruders.

The most important room in the entire complex was the Blue Séance Room, for it was here that Sarah communicated with the good spirits who were her friends. None of Sarah's large staff of servants were ever allowed to enter this windowless sanctum with walls of blue. In fact, almost no one had the faintest idea where the seance room was hidden.

Each evening at sunset, Sarah ordered the head butler to go to the base of the bell tower and pull the long cord that rang the Spirit Bell. While the tolling bell summoned the spirits, the mystic little lady traipsed off through the meandering, dark corridors until she reached a barely noticeable wall panel. After glancing about to be sure she was unobserved, she pressed a concealed button causing the panel to slide open. One quick step and she was inside her secret chamber.

The Blue Séance Room was the most sparsely furnished room in the mansion. A large lantern in a Tiffany glass lampshade cast a soft circle of light on a round hardwood table. At this table, Sarah seated herself in a highbacked armchair and awaited the arrival of her ghostly guests.

They came to her as spots of light, she told her only confidant, Margaret Merriam. Then, they turned into wavering, luminous human figures and gathered around the table. There were 12 in all —an even dozen phantoms, both male and female. Each night, they discussed new architectural plans with Sarah, suggesting designs for additional rooms, hallways and cellars. Sarah carefully recorded their instructions in a large notebook, and, in the morning, ordered her crew of 22 carpenters to commence carrying out the spirits' wishes.

When the business part of the séance ended, the tiny woman rose from her chair and led the fluorescent apparitions down a secret passage to *Llanada Villa's* main dining room. Here, a long table had been set for thirteen, with a lavish feast set upon it. Nothing but the best was good enough for Sarah's spectral companions. Caviar, pheasant under glass, Oysters Rockefeller, and minted roast loins of lamb graced the table. Bottles of fine wine stood ready to be poured into crystal glasses.

No servants were permitted in the great hall while Madam dined, but after she finished her meal and went on to her Grand Ballroom, they came in to clear the table. Sarah's plate was always empty, but the other 12 dishes were still piled high with food. The waiters shook their heads as they carried the plates away, but, as Sarah explained to Margaret, the spirits only dined on the spirit of the food, leaving it seemingly untouched.

After dinner, Sarah sat down at the beautiful rosewood grand piano in her gleaming ballroom and played light-hearted melodies while the incandescent wraiths twirled around the dance floor. When the dancing ended, the good spirits departed, and Sarah went off to bed. She slept in a different room every night so the bad spirits would not know where to find her and would get lost searching for her.

It was —and still is— very easy to get lost in *Llanada Villa.* An incident which occurred in the late 1890s illustrates how frightening this could be.

A young woman named María had taken a job in

the mansion as a member of the large cleaning staff. She fervently wished to make a good impression during her first day on the job so she worked as hard as she could scrubbing and polishing the endless, tile-floored corridors. By quitting time, María had worked her way well out of sight of her co-workers.

Justifiably alarmed, she dashed back down the hallway, making one wrong turn after another until she lost all sense of direction. María ran deeper into the unfamiliar house, opening doors and stumbling through deserted rooms. Twilight was dimming the stained glass windows when, at last, she began following a long, narrow passageway in the heart of the mansion.

María was groping her way along the wall when her outstretched hand accidentally pressed a barely noticeable button next to a smoothly recessed wall panel. The panel slid open, and María found herself in a doorway, face to face with the mistress of the house.

Sarah Winchester rose with a gasp from behind her séance table. "What are you doing here?", she shrieked. "My god, girl! You could have led the evil spirits to me. Get out! Get out!"

Poor María dashed away in a state of near panic, fleeing like a trapped bird until she finally reached two etched glass French doors which opened onto a garden. With a great sigh of relief, she ran breathlessly through the flowerbeds to the outer gate and on down the palm-lined street beyond.

In the morning, a very nervous María returned to *Llanada Villa* but, at the employee's entrance, a stern-faced Charles Farnham awaited her. "Madam Winchester has instructed me to inform you that your employment has been terminated," he said. He reached into this coat pocket and withdrew a fat envelope. "She has also authorized the payment of six months' wages on the condition that you never, ever set foot on this property again."

María gratefully accepted the money and, probably not too reluctantly, went on her way.

Sarah Winchester was well known for both her strictness and her generosity toward her employees. At a time when two dollars was considered a good daily wage, Sarah paid her workers between three and five dollars per day. Many of her employees received far more than that; her offers of extremely high salaries lured some of Europe's finest chefs to San Jose from Paris and Vienna, and her talented team of gardeners had come all the way from Japan.

As the years went by, Sarah not only continued to build, but she also constantly modernized the existing sections of the mansion. Each new technological innovation that came along was quickly incorporated into the great house. An electrical generator was installed so light bulbs could replace the gaslamps, and elevators could rise from floor to floor. *Llanada Villa*'s heating, water and sewer systems were always state of the art.

When automobiles became popular, Sarah traded in her horse-drawn carriages for two Pierce Arrow limousines. Farnham had retired by this time so Sarah hired two equally dignified automobile drivers. However, these chauffeurs had little to do beyond keeping the cars polished since their employer rarely went anywhere.

Upon occasion, Sarah did get the urge to do a bit of shopping. Even then, she never set foot on the streets of San Jose. The grand matron always remained in her limousine while the shopkeepers brought their merchandise out to the curb for her inspection. Once she had made her selections, she ordered the goods to be delivered to the service entrance of the mansion.

When Sarah reached her eighties, she no longer left the house at all and, in 1922, she died in her sleep in her favorite bedroom. Her will named her niece and personal secretary, Margaret Merriam Marriott, as the new owner of *Llanada Villa*, specified that all long-term employees would receive ample pensions, and that the rest of her immense fortune be given to charities.

Margaret Marriott was also quite elderly by this time and lacked the energy needed to maintain and supervise the huge estate. Within a year, she sold it to a wealthy businessman, T.C. Barnett. Eventually, the property came into the ownership of a private corporation which opened the mansion to the general public as a tourist attraction.

Now, on a daily basis, thousands of curiosity seekers follow tour guides through the innermost recesses of Sarah Winchester's once-secret haven. As they listen to the strange stories of the old woman's alleged rapport with the spirit world, they cannot help but wonder if this rambling, museum-like house really is haunted.

Did twelve benevolent ghosts once dine and dance here? If so, do they still make appearances on the premises? And the most intriguing question of all: did Sarah join them after her death? Are there now 13 spirits in *Llanada Villa*?

There is every reason to believe that Mrs. Winchester expected to become the thirteenth spirit. The number 13 is repeated over and over throughout the mansion. There are 13 lights on each ballroom chandelier, 13 steps to the thirteenth bathroom and

13 panes in a row of 13 windows. Many stairways
have 13 steps, and 13 palm trees line the front drive-
way. The Spirit Bell was always rung 13 times each
evening, and Sarah's will was signed 13 times.

Psychic phenomena has been reported on a regular basis during the years since Sarah's demise. A
nebulous light is often observed above the bed where
she died; faint piano music is sometimes heard, and
soft voices whisper in the Blue Séance Room. Frequently, doors and windows open and close by themselves, and lights turn back on after they have been
shut off.

Naturally, the Winchester Mystery House has
drawn a good many psychics into its spooky interior.
These clairvoyant people have repeatedly witnessed
floating lights, discovered "cold spots" in some of the
rooms and have tape recorded barely audible piano
music.

Numerous séances have been held in the Blue
Séance Room, always with astonishing results. Psychic Silvia Brown, co-founder of the Nirvana Foundation, conducted a remarkable session in the early
1970s. Accompanied by four other people including a
San Francisco newspaperwoman, Antoinette May,
Brown's psychic efforts brought forth a display of red
lights which seemed to almost explode before they
faded away.

Probably, the most extraordinary —and frightening— séance of all occurred at midnight on Halloween
in 1975.

Jeanne Bergen, a paranormal investigator from
Pinole, California, was the medium. Prior to the
séance, Bergen toured the quiet, empty house. As
she stood meditatively beside the bed where Sarah
died, an indistinct white face appeared momentarily

on the wall. Bergen therefore insisted that the séance be held in Sarah's bedroom.

A large, round table was placed near the foot of the bed, and six people (three psychics and three reporters) seated themselves around it. Bergen went into a deep trance. While everyone sat in silence, the room grew very cold.

Then, to the amazement of all, Jeanne Bergen's face began to age visibly. Her hair turned gray, and deep lines appeared on her forehead. She started trembling and gasping for breath. With wrinkled, age-spotted hands, she clutched at her chest as she slumped out of her chair onto the floor.

Her horrified companions quickly carried her out of the frigid room and into the warm hallway, where her breathing soon returned to normal, and the signs of old age disappeared. Bergen could only say that her body had been possessed by someone else; someone who was dying. She believed she had somehow experienced the same heart attack that killed Sarah Winchester.

Sarah has been dead now for more than 70 years. Yet, her spirit is still very much an invisible presence in the Winchester mansion. One hopes she is not an unhappy ghost, that she is now at ease and free from fear. Still, she may well be quite resentful of the irreverent parades of sightseers tramping daily through her once inviolate sanctuary. Perhaps, now she hides not from malevolent spirits but from tittering tourists.

On the other hand, Sarah Winchester may be much too busy to worry about such trivial goings-on. Chances are, she is still playing the role of the perfect hostess when her 12 friends drop by to see her every night.

How to Tour the Winchester Mystery House

The Winchester Mansion is located in San Jose at 525 Winchester Boulevard between Steven Creek Boulevard and I-280. Guided tours are conducted all day every day starting at 9 am, except on Christmas Day. Included are Mansion Interior Tours of 110 of the 160 rooms, and spooky after-dark Flashlight Tours. Be sure to stay close to your tour guide.

Bibliography - Chapter 2

Edson, K.R. *True West* magazine. Austin, Texas. Western Publications, Inc. May-June, 1963.

Holbrook, Marion R. *Frontier Times* magazine. Austin, Texas. Western Publications, Inc. October, 1985.

Murray, Earl. **Ghosts of the Old West**. New York. Dorset Press. 1988.

Myers, Arthur. **The Ghostly Register**. Chicago. Contemporary Books, Inc. 1986.

Roberts, Nancy. **Haunted Houses: Tales From 30 American Homes**. Chester, Connecticut. The Globe Pequot Press. 1988.

3

A Ghostly Tour of
Haunted Hotels

California is a perfect place to go exploring
haunted houses. Not only are there plenty of them,
but several are, like the Winchester Mansion, open to
the public. There is nothing more exhilarating than
roaming the lonely corridors of an old, classic hotel
knowing a ghost may be encountered at any moment.
Nothing is more deliciously scary than spending a
night in a room known to be haunted. And in Califor-

nia there are plenty of opportunities to do exactly that.

One of the state's most popular haunted houses is San Diego's Horton Grand. Its mysterious Room 309 is always booked up months in advance by people willing to pay over $100 a night to scare themselves half silly. In fact, any room on the third floor is eagerly sought out by ghost seekers since pale apparitions have been seen in the hallways many times.

Room 309, however, is definitely the center of the luxurious hotel's psychic activity. A diary is available in the room at all times and the entries penned by the guests make astonishing reading.

The most common phenomenon is the rearranging of pictures on the walls. Guests have returned to the room to find all of the previously perfectly-hung pictures tilted at odd angles, or, in at least one case, hanging upside down. Lights turn on and off for no apparent reason and the door often locks itself from the inside.

Much more frightening are the physical contacts with a ghost. Guests —particularly women— have reported being awakened by something tugging on their arms, trying to draw them from the bed. One of these guests was a San Diego businesswoman, Chris McGuire.

McGuire had reserved the infamous room for the night of her birthday, December 14, in 1987. After dinner with friends, she returned to 309, and with a companion, turned in for the night. Along about midnight, something awakened her by touching her arm.

McGuire sat up with a start and called out to her friend, Helen Martinez, who was sleeping in the next bed. The two women turned on the light but no one was in the room. Within the hour, McGuire experienced the touch again, but, as before, no one was there. Then, at 2:30 am, the touch became a grasp and pulled on her arm as the bed began to vibrate. McGuire opened her eyes to see a misty figure of a man tugging on her arm.

She cried out, and the figure evaporated and was gone. Needless to say, the rest of the night passed very slowly.

Other guests have had equally eerie experiences on the third floor of the Horton Grand. Once, a mother emerged from the bathroom in 309 to find her little daughter engaged in an animated conversation with an invisible new friend. On another occasion, a woman left her room to search for the third floor ice machine. Spotting a tall, dark-suited man waiting for the elevator, she asked for directions. The man turned, stared at her, and faded away.

Naturally, Room 309 draws psychics by the dozens. Invariably, these super-sensitive people find a night spent in the spooky, locked room to be immensely rewarding. The ceiling fan turns on, faint laughter is heard but cannot be recorded, and some guests returning to the room have found all of the coat hangers flung out across the floor.

The psychics believe the room is inhabited or visited frequently by at least three ghosts. The adult ghost is an early San Diego resident named Roger Whittaker, a shady character about whom little is known for certain. He may have been a professional gambler. Or a pimp. Or both.

The other two are juveniles. One has given his name to psychic Shelly Deegan as "Henry." The other calls himself "Gus." Henry was a teenager when he died; Gus was only 12. They were friends and worked together in a hotel, though Deegan cannot determine where or when.

Whittaker is the most intriguing of the three since his life and death can in no way be connected to the Horton Grand. Deegan believes Whittaker was shot to death in 1843. Apparently, he was pursued by the father of a girl whose virtue he had stolen. The father discovered Whittaker hiding in an ornate armoire and promptly avenged his daughter's honor.

The armoire could not have been in a room at the Horton Grand. The original hotel was not built until 1886, during the boom that followed the arrival of the first transcontinental railroad. The Horton Grand —then known as the Grand Horton— was truly a showplace in its time. During the 1920s, it played host to Babe Ruth and Jack Dempsey, George Raft and George Jessel. Its magnificence lasted nearly a 100 years, but by 1980, it was looking shabby and neglected.

In 1981, a foresighted San Diego entrepreneur, Dan Pearson, purchased the aged hotel, dismantled it into 10,000 pieces, and rebuilt it at its present location. This move raises an interesting question: Did the ghosts reside in the original hotel and move with it to its new locale? Or did they check in after the hotel was reconstructed? These questions cannot be answered because no ghosts ever registered at the front desk.

When one goes ghost hunting in old San Diego, a visit to the Whaley House Museum is mandatory. This grand old house is so full of ghosts that the United States Chamber of Commerce has "authenticated" it as being "genuinely haunted." The mansion's inexplicable phenomena were further investigated in a September, 1994 episode of Fox Television's "Sightings" series.

In order for a house to be declared haunted at least one of several phenomena must occur on a regular basis. Unaccountable lights must be seen, unlikely sounds such as footsteps or tapping noises must be heard or "cold spots" must be felt. Inanimate objects will move about without cause, out-of-place odors will be smelled, or the presence of apparitions will be sensed and sometimes seen.

According to the museum's curator, June Reading, every one of these diverse phenomena occurs in the Whaley House from time to time.

The history of Whaley House is rather unique. It was built on the site of the town's old gallows, where, in 1851, a particularly grisly hanging took place. The victim was a drifter known as Yankee Jim, who was arrested for attempting to steal a boat. At the time, San Diego was under martial law, and "justice" was often brutally harsh. Jim was sentenced to be hanged.

Capital punishment seems a bit severe for such a small crime, but by men who valued their boats the way other westerners valued their horses, the sentence was deemed appropriate. Yankee Jim was taken to the gallows and it is said he as so sure he would be pardoned at the last minute that he laughed and joked until the noose was placed around his neck. The hanging was badly bungled and Jim took nearly an hour to die.

Thomas Whaley, a prominent local businessman, bought the land in 1856 and built his home upon it. His house was unique in many ways. It was the first all-brick building in San Diego, done in an eastern style to please his New Yorker wife, Anna. Originally, an unfloored granary adjoined the residence, and in 1869, Whaley converted this space into a courtroom which served San Diego County for the next two years.

Later, the room was used variously as a city hall, a church, a public school, a post office, and a theatre.

Anna Whaley bore and raised six children. One day, a little friend of one of her daughters, Annabelle Washburn, ran merrily into the back yard, hit a clothesline, and broke her neck. Thomas carried her into the house and she died in the kitchen, not far from the spot where the gallows once stood.

Thomas Whaley himself died in 1890 at age 67, and Anna passed on in 1913. The Whaley's youngest daughter, a spinster named Lillian, lived her entire life in Whaley House, dying at age 89 in 1953.

By now, the aging mansion was badly deteriorated. The paint was peeling, the upper windows were boarded up, and the second-story porch was mostly fallen away. Talk was circulating about razing the old relic to make way for a modern structure. Then, in 1956, a group of concerned San Diegans organized the Historical Shrine Foundation of San Diego. They raised enough funds to purchase the property and lobbied the County into restoring the house as a museum.

It was during the restoration that the haunted nature of the house emerged. Early one morning, Curator June Reading was discussing plans with some workers on the ground floor when heavy footsteps creaked on the boards of the second floor. Thinking a carpenter had arrived early, Reading climbed the stairs only to find the upper rooms completely empty.

This phenomenon repeated itself over and over, usually in front of multiple witnesses. The thud of footsteps like those of a large man wearing boots echoed across the second floor and sometimes came partway down the stairs. No one was ever seen.

Once, Reading was accompanied by a charming young tour guide, Denise Pournelle, and they investigated the sounds. While they explored the empty second floor rooms, a deep baritone laugh resounded around them. The women were terrified. "We both went 'lickety out' of the house," Reading said later.

Strange odors have also permeated the place; both the feminine scent of perfume and the masculine scent of cigars have been detected.

In the kitchen, there is often the smell of food cooking although nothing is on the stove. Once in awhile, children report seeing a little girl in the kitchen.

The apparitions of Whaley House are particularly fascinating since, upon occasion, they have been photographed —and identified.

During one Christmas season, the museum's staff decorated the courtroom tree with old fashioned ornaments and popcorn ropes, then posed in front of it for a group picture. When the film was developed, the print revealed a diminutive woman dressed in a long, 19th century dress standing at the edge of the group. It was unmistakably Anna Whaley whose portrait hangs in the living room.

Thomas Whaley, too, has accidentally been captured on film. Invariably, he is bearded, wears a dark top hat and a full length, black frock coat. He is also sighted sometimes, usually outdoors, standing behind some ferns, looking toward his mansion. A third man was once caught in the background of a Polaroid snapshot and is believed to be Yankee Jim, because his clothes and appearance are rather coarse.

Even stranger things have been photographed in Whaley House. A tourist from New Jersey once took a picture of the judge's bench, which he immediately showed to June Reading. Across the bench was an image of something which she could only describe as "an energy form. It was cloudy and white, about eight inches across. It looked like a big, heavy piece of yarn." Later, Reading would witness two of these manifestations herself.

On a summer afternoon in the late 1980s, she noticed there was an unusual amount of static electricity throughout the museum. Around three o'clock, a visitor called her upstairs to see something he had discovered in one of the children's rooms. "Something like fireflies was flying around," she said.

Reading called the Parapsychology Foundation, described what she was seeing and was told it was probably "ectoplasmic tubes," the substance from which the ghostly figures form if enough tubes are present. Reading went back again to watch the strange display, and sure enough, half a human figure formed at the end of the bed; its arms were folding clothes or doing some similar household chore.

Not long after this occurred, Reading began seeing an ectoplasm form in the study from time to time. Filmy and misty, it expanded and contracted but never developed into a specific shape. It simply hovered directly over Thomas Whaley's desk.

Whaley's house is full of wonders, and the past has been recreated in meticulous detail. From the sparkling crystal chandeliers to the dark, polished wood of a Jenny Lind piano, an antique world is on display. But the fact that people from a by-gone era are also present makes the Whaley House Museum even more enthralling.

Across the San Diego Bay, the sumptuous Hotel del Cornonado is said to host a ghost in Room 3502. But that elusive phantom is seen by few and only under specific weather conditions.

The hotel's management denies the existence of the ghost but enough people have seen it to make the spectre impossible to dismiss. The grand seaside resort has faced the mighty Pacific since 1888. Above its white sand beaches and blue water marina, this tall, red-roofed compound has entertained several generations of the rich and famous. Its domed dining rooms, garden courtyards, and picturesque gazebos have charmed America's elite for over a century.

The legend of the Hotel del Coronado's ghost is hard to pin down. What actually happened in Room 3502 on a fateful night in 1892 will never be precisely agreed upon, but the psychic aftermath has not been explained away.

The identity of the young woman who died so tragically in the hotel seems to be established as Kate Garrou, the wife of a roving gambler. Her husband, Lou, was a rambling man. During the early years of their marriage, he made an honest attempt to settle down and stop wandering. But the lure of the road was too strong. Lou Garrou could not resist the allure of the casinos in San Francisco, Sacramento, and San Diego. Before long, he was leaving Kate alone in their Los Angeles home for longer and longer periods of time.

Finally, the inevitable day came when Kate received a letter, written on Hotel del Coronado stationery, asking for a divorce. In desperation, Kate packed a suitcase, and as a wild afterthought, tossed in a small, pearl-handled revolver before heading off to Coronado.

Stormy winds were blowing in off of the Pacific when she arrived. Kate caught her breath in the lobby before going up to her husband's room, where, just as she expected, she found him with another woman. Knowing her marriage was finished now for sure, she stumbled away, brokenhearted.

The storm had hit the resort with its full fury. Rain was pouring down, so Kate checked into a room on the third floor. As lightning flashed, she wrote a suicide note, took out the little revolver and pressed it to her right temple.

Due to the trembling of her hand, the shot she fired was not instantly fatal. Kate Garrou staggered, crying and bleeding, to collapse and die in the rain. It was a death scene that scores of hotel guests claim is repeated over and over each time a heavy storm hits the hotel.

Guests, hurrying back to their rooms through the downpour, have repeatedly been shocked to see the crumpled, sodden body of a young woman lying near the door of Room 3502. When they screamed, the body always vanished. So, perhaps, when it rains at Hotel del Coronado, it is best just to stay indoors.

Another troubled hotel ghost resides in Ione, a small town southeast of Sacramento. This spirit is seeking help from the living but there is no way help can be given. The hotel and the ghost date back to the Gold Rush era. Hotel Ione is neither as large nor as splendid as most of the hotels in those days but it is so authentically Western it looks just like a movie set. Millie and William Jones purchased and renovated Hotel Ione in 1977. On June 22 of that year, Millie had her first encounter with an apparition that would puzzle her for months to come.

That afternoon as she went about performing

HOTEL DEL CORONADO. Today's guests still scream when they encounter a frontier gambler's heartbroken wife dying in the rain.

Hotel brochure photograph

her chores, she entered the dining room and confronted a column of what appeared to be white smoke. The smoky cloud was about the same height and shape as a human being. It hovered but did not drift. Thinking something was burning, Jones waved a napkin at the smoke. It dissipated briefly but quickly resumed its original form. Millie Jones called in the dishwasher and together they stared at the frightening phenomenon until it faded away.

Although shaken, Jones continued to prepare the dining room for the dinner crowd. After placing candles on each table, she went to the kitchen to pick up silverware and napkins. Upon her return, every candle in the room had lighted itself. Quickly, she extinguished them only to have them re-light the moment she turned her back.

This phenomenon reoccurred each time candles were placed on the tables; every night, the candles burned until they were tiny, flickering flames in a pool of wax. By now, Jones was reasonably, though reluctantly, sure she and her husband had a ghost on their hands. But what kind of ghost? Why did this particular spirit constantly manifest itself in smoke and fire? To attempt to answer this question, Millie called in a psychic friend, an elderly woman who claimed to be able to communicate with the dead.

The old woman arranged for a séance in the hotel dining room. One night after closing time, six hotel employees gathered around a table in the darkened dining room and a candle was placed in the center. It immediately lighted itself. As everyone sat silently in the dim circle of light, the medium spoke softly, "We know you are here. Who are you?"

There was no response so she asked again, "Who are you?" Millie Jones, who was holding a pen above a piece of paper, suddenly wrote, "Mary Phelps."

The medium asked, "Why are you here, Mary Phelps?" and Millie's hand, of its own accord, wrote, "My baby's in a fire. Help me!"

"What room are you in?" the old woman asked calmly. Millie's hand swung back and forth wildly as if the ghost controlling her was confused and did not know the answer. Then, at last, Millie wrote "Baby Jon." The pen fell from her fingers and the spell of the séance was broken.

Millie Jones knew from the restoration work that there once had been a fire in a second floor room. Had Mary Phelps' baby, Jon, perished in that fire? A full year would pass before she would receive an answer to that question.

In October of 1978, a woman from Calaveras County dined at Hotel Ione. Following the meal, she told Millie that she had heard there was a ghost in the hotel named Mary Phelps. "My great-grandmother's name was Mary Phelps. She wrote in her diary that she lost her little son, Jon, in a hotel room fire in 1884. Perhaps this was the hotel."

Perhaps it was. Further confirmation came in 1980 when a couple from Sacramento were awakened in a second floor room by a small, young woman wearing a long, black dress and white bonnet. She was hysterically imploring them to get her baby out of a fire. Possibly she is doomed to live that terrible night again and again throughout eternity.

All of California's hotel ghosts seem destined to relive their most traumatic moments endlessly. Unlike the living guests, they never check out and move on. The hotels' ghosts are permanent residents. All other guests are simply temporary intruders.

How to Visit
California's Haunted Hotels

San Diego's Horton Grand Hotel stands proudly at 311 Island Street in Old Chinatown, three blocks from the waterfront.Whaley House is located at 2482 San Diego Avenue and is open daily except major holidays. Hotel del Coronado is reached by crossing San Diego Bay on Highway 75 to 1500 Orange Avenue. To visit Hotel Ione, take Interstate 5 south from Sacramento to Highway 104; then go east for 24 miles to 41 Main Street in Ione. The ambiance can be appreciated whether spooks are active or not.

Bibliography - Chapter 3

Holbrook, Marion R. **Frontier Times**. Austin, Texas. Western Publications. October, 1985.

Murray, Earl. **Ghosts of the Old West**. New York. Dorset Press. 1988.

Myers, Arthur. *The Ghostly Register*. Chicago. Contemporary Books, Inc. 1986.

Myers, Arthur. **The Ghostly Gazetteer**. Chicago. Contemporary Books, Inc. 1990

Reading, June. **The Whaley House**. San Diego. Historical Shrine Foundation. 1993.

Roberts, Nancy. **Haunted Houses. Tales From 30 American Homes**. Chester, Connecticut. The Globe Pequot Press. 1988.

4

Ghosts of the Movie Stars

Stardom is a form of immortality. No movie star ever seems to really die, for, unlike other mortals, they continue to live on in their films. Years after their physical deaths, their fans can still see them as they were in life, still very much alive on the silver screen.

However, a number of movie stars have left more behind than images on celluloid. Some say that several of Hollywood's greatest actors and actresses have come back from their graves as ghosts. They have returned, time and again, to the places they loved best, to the mansions, grand estates and yachts where they had known their greatest happiness.

Rudolf Valentino was one of the first.

Valentino was the greatest matinee idol of his time, adored by millions of women worldwide. Darkly handsome and gracefully lithe, Valentino caused women to faint in movie theatres when he turned his smoldering, melancholy gaze on his heroines. He aroused hidden desires for forbidden love that were otherwise suppressed except in fantasies. Rudolf Valentino became every woman's secret lover.

Like most early movie stars, Valentino climbed the ladder of success from the bottom rung. Born in 1895 to an Italian family of modest means, he traveled to Paris at the age of 17. Unable to find work, he wound up begging for coins on the streets. A year later, he made his way to New York where he again lived on the fringes of society —washing dishes and waiting tables. He was arrested several times for petty theft.

Valentino was always a superb dancer. In 1915, he wisely changed his name from Rudolfo Alfonso Raffaele Philibert Guglielmi to Rudolf Valentino and became a taxi dancer in the city's dancehalls and night clubs. Soon, the agile young man began landing small parts in Broadway musicals and became committed to show business.

The summer of 1918 found him knocking on the doors of Hollywood's casting offices, accepting any bit parts available as a tango dancer or a sleazy villain. His breakthrough came in 1921 when he was given the lead in Rex Ingram's silent epic, *The Four Horsemen of the Apocalypse*. The movie was a tremendous box office success and Rudolf Valentino became a superstar over night.

The young, once-penniless Italian immigrant had achieved fame and adoration, wealth, and acclaim beyond his wildest dreams. And then —suddenly— he was dead.

On August 24, 1926 at the age of 31, Rudolf Valentino was rushed to a New York hospital with a perforated ulcer. Though hundreds of tearful female fans held a vigil outside, he did not last the night.

Valentino's death sent a shock wave across the nation; several suicides were reported and a near riot ensued during his funeral procession when the thousands of women lining the route surged forward, trying to touch the passing hearse. Almost as quickly as he came on the scene, Valentino was gone, to be mourned for decades by his faithful, devoted fan clubs.

One year before his death, Valentino had purchased a $175,000, 16 room mansion for his wife, Natasha Rambova. It was a magnificent estate: a white, tile roofed Spanish-style compound of adjoining buildings arranged around a wide, lantern-lit, tree shaded courtyard lush with bougainvillaea. The actor named his villa Falcon Lair, the title of an upcoming film he would never make.

Shortly after Rudolf's death, Natasha put the estate up for sale. The realtors who showed the mansion to their wealthy clients, however, soon began complaining nervously about a ghostly presence in the house. Eerie sounds came from the empty rooms and footsteps often echoed down long corridors. Several realtors became so frightened they refused to continue showing the place.

In 1927, the fabulously wealthy Standard Oil heiress, Millicent Rogers, rented Falcon Lair for three months with an option to buy. She spent one night in the mansion and never returned. Rogers told her friends she had rounded a turn in a hallway and came face to face with Rudolf Valentino. As she stumbled backwards in fright, Valentino walked toward her, his arms outstretched and a look of longing in his eyes. Rogers locked herself in a nearby bedroom, turned on every light and sat there trembling the rest of the night.

Soon, others began reporting sightings. Most often, Valentino was seen striding dramatically across the courtyard dressed as a Spanish *gaucho*. Once, at twilight, a caretaker walked into Falcon Lair's stables just in time to see Rudolf petting his favorite horse. Sometimes, tourists who stood outside the locked gates claimed to hear 1920s style music drifting out of the dark, empty mansion. Rudolf Valentino never disappointed his admirers. As a phantom, he lingered on at Falcon Lair until the last of his faithful fans had been laid to rest.

One of Valentino's most distinguished contemporaries was renowned actor Clifton Webb. Webb's life paralleled Valentino's in several respects; he began his career as a dancer, went on to become a popular actor, and, after his death, returned to haunt his mansion.

Born in 1891 with the cumbersome name of Webb Parmalee Hollenbeck, the handsome young man became a leading ballroom dancer at the age of 19. His most illustrious partner was a lovely woman named Bonnie Glass, who, after Webb went on to the Broadway stage, became Valentino's dancing partner.

In 1920, Clifton Webb began appearing in silent movies but it was not until 1944 that he struck it big with an Academy Award nomination for best supporting actor in Otto Preminger's *Laura*. Two years later, he was again nominated for his supporting role in *The Razor's Edge*. Now, Clifton Webb could definitely afford a mansion of his own.

The house he chose was a grand one, even by Beverly Hills standards. It is a multi-terraced house of grey stucco with wrought iron balconies. Tall Corinthian columns guard the ornate French doors, giving the mansion a stately, palatial appearance.

Webb had not lived long in the manor before he discovered that the ghost of the previous owner was still in residence. The house had been built in the 1930s by opera star and actress Grace Moore. This gifted soprano had captivated audiences at the Metropolitan Opera and in movie theatres across the nation. Like many stars who became ghosts, she died a sudden death, in a plane crash over Copenhagen during a 1944 European tour.

Apparently, her spirit decided to return to the comforts of her mansion and it seemed Clifton Webb had no objections to her frequent appearances, as he lived in the haunted house for more than 20 years.

Clifton Webb never married; he shared his home with his mother, Maybelle Hollenbeck. When Maybelle died in 1960, Clifton often saw her ghost in her room. Webb made sure his mother's clothes and all her favorite things were kept exactly as she left them so she would always feel at home.

When Webb himself died in October of 1966, he joined the other ghosts in his great mansion. The new owners, producer Douglas Crammer and his wife, columnist Joyce Haber, soon became aware of his presence. Whenever they hosted a party, someone invariably asked, "Who is that distinguished looking man standing near the doorway? Oh dear, he's gone. But he was there a moment ago."

Before long, the new owners themselves began seeing the ghost of Clifton Webb. Every so often, they entered a closed-off room in time to see a tall, misty figure pacing back and forth, repeating "Well, well, well." This, they found out later, was a favorite expression of Webb's. Clifton Webb was an adamant nonsmoker; he absolutely detested cigarettes. Both Haber and Crammer learned not to leave their smokes laying around the house, as they would inevitably find them crushed and shredded.

One of Webb's most surprising appearances occurred when a maid glanced out a window and saw the actor on the other side of the glass, looking in. "It was him, all right," the maid told her employers. "He was dressed just like he was when he played that snooty old Mr. Belvedere."

Many of Hollywood's ghosts do seem to enjoy replaying their favorite movie roles. The ghost of Buster Keaton, for example, could only be the spirit of a man who lived his life as a comedian. It seems only natural that Keaton might return as a prank-playing poltergeist.

Buster Keaton was one of the most artful and innovative comics of the silent screen. The character he created and perfected remained constant throughout most of his long career. He was always the "little guy," a bewildered, hapless soul adrift in a confusing, hostile world. Still, he always prevailed in the end. He survived all adversities through resourcefulness, bravery and silliness. Whether he was running like a squirrel in a cage inside a riverboat paddle wheel or was caught up in a runaway hot air balloon or simply trying to assemble a house from a do-it-yourself kit, his plights always evoked as much sympathy as laughter.

Between 1917 and 1923, Keaton appeared in 37 classic "two-reelers" —short comedies 20 minutes each in length. In the years that followed, he made 51 feature films and 25 more shorts. As often as not, he wrote screenplays and directed the pictures as well.

His house was truly a magnificent one, an Italian white stucco villa with red tile roofs set on beautifully landscaped grounds. When Keaton died in 1966 at the age of 71, his mansion was purchased by television comedian Dick Christie and his wife, Chris.

Almost immediately after they moved in, the Christies started experiencing odd phenomena in the house. Whenever either of them got up during the night, the hall light would turn itself on for them. When they returned to the bedroom, the light would click off. The first time it happened, the frightened couple lay awake the rest of the night, fearing a prowler in the mansion.

One morning, Dick Christie got up early to make some important calls but found the phone was dead. Upon checking, he discovered both telephones were unplugged. This was especially mystifying since the last thing Christie had done before going to bed was take an incoming call.

Other capricious tricks were played almost nightly. Ceiling fans suddenly started turning in empty rooms; door bells sometimes rang when no one was at the door and drapes that had been closed for the night were wide open at dawn.

The Christies invited a prominent parapsychologist, Dr. Erik Marten of the European Institute of Psychic Research, to tour their enchanted villa. Marten concluded that there was little doubt the strange phenomena was being caused by the ghost of Buster Keaton. "Playing with lights and unplugging phones would be completely in character for him," Dr. Marten said.

The later years of Keaton's life had not been happy ones. His wife divorced him, he lapsed into alcoholism, entered a psychiatric clinic for a time and was largely unappreciated by a new generation of movie goers. "Perhaps, his poltergeist antics are a way of letting it be known that he is happy again, contented with his life as a spirit," Martens speculated.

One Beverly Hills ghost who definitely does not seem to be happy in the spirit world is the "Blonde Bombshell" of the 1930s, Jean Harlow. Those who have seen or felt her ethereal presence in her former home believe she is emanating a deep sense of sorrow. This may well be, for her brief life was marred by tragedy.

Jean Harlow was once the most stunningly sensual woman in Hollywood. Her platinum blonde hair, breathtaking beauty, and sultry voice made her the epitome of glamour.

She got her start in 1928, when, at the age of 17, she began working as an extra in silent comedies. With the advent of talking pictures, Harlow landed the lead in Howard Hughes' aviation saga *Hell's Angels* and was on her way to stardom. Before long, she was being cast alongside the leading stars of her day, Clark Gable and Spencer Tracy.

The critics usually panned her acting but her audiences loved her. Soon, Jean Harlow became to men what Rudolf Valentino had been to women.

In 1932, Harlow married producer/director Paul Bern, a man twice her age. They moved into a fine house with tall chimneys and flagstoned archways. Only two months after the wedding, Bern's body was found in his bathtub; a pistol and suicide note lay on the floor next to him. In the note, he admitted impotence and hinted that his wife's ridicule had led him to take his life.

Harlow weathered the storm of scathingly bad publicity that followed her husband's shocking death and continued to make motion pictures. In 1933, she remarried to Harold Rossen, a director of photography. This union lasted less than a year. Her next lover was a suave, popular leading man, William Powell. Their relationship was also stormy and tempestuous, resulting in an engagement but a forever postponed marriage.

Jean Harlow's star continued to shine brightly but her personal life was a shambles. Then, unexpectedly, it came swiftly to an end. She was hospitalized in 1937 for uremia and died shortly after of cerebral edema. She was only 26.

Her spirit has been seen repeatedly ever since, usually late at night. She is seen standing at a window or sitting alone in a darkened room, always looking sad and sometimes weeping mournfully.

Many spirits find no joy in the otherworld, and Jean Harlow is certainly one of them. But there is another actress whose after-life happiness is likely in doubt. Like Harlow, she, too, was a Hollywood sex goddess, perhaps the most famous of them all. Her name is Marilyn Monroe.

Though she almost perpetually wore a beguiling smile, Monroe's entire life was a sad one. Her sudden, untimely death shocked her fans and remains shrouded in mystery to this day. Her apparition has been seen at least once since she died but those who witnessed this incredible manifestation gained no new insights about the mysterious nature of her death.

As most of her millions of admirers know, Marilyn Monroe was born Norma Jean Baker Mortenson in Los Angeles in 1926. Norma Jean never knew her father; he deserted her mother, Gladys, before Norma was born. Gladys Mortenson suffered a nervous breakdown and was institutionalized in 1931, leaving Norma Jean to spend her childhood in a series of foster homes and an orphanage.

When Norma Jean reached the age of 16, her

aunt, Grace, suggested that an early marriage might be the best way for her to lead a more stable life. Dutifully, Norma Jean married the man her aunt chose for her, 18 year old Jim Dougherty.

It was wartime so Dougherty soon joined the merchant marine and went overseas. During his absence, Norma Jean took a job in a defense plant. There, in that unlikely setting, a series of photographs were taken that would change her life forever.

A photographer from the Army's Pictorial Center in Hollywood arrived one day to shoot pictures of the workers for use as "morale boosters" in the armed service's newspapers. He was so impressed by the young parachute inspector's photogenic beauty that he showed pictures of her to the largest modeling agency in Los Angeles. Norma Jean soon found herself working as a model. Before long a screen test followed and the now-blonde Norma Jean Dougherty became a starlet named Marilyn Monroe.

She went from bit parts to stardom in just five years but fame and fortune did not bring her happiness. Inwardly, she remained insecure and vulnerable. Marilyn had long since divorced Jim Dougherty, who disagreed with her choice of careers, and now there were many men in her life. One of them was a young U.S. senator from Massachusetts, John F. Kennedy.

According to most accounts, Kennedy asked his brother-in-law, actor Peter Lawford, to introduce him to the stunning new actress. Their relationship may have been casual at first, but the two charismatic people felt their attraction intensify over the years.

In 1952, during a quick trip to Mexico, Marilyn impulsively married a newspaper correspondent, Robert Slatzer. They annulled their marriage within a week but continued to be lifelong friends. It was this

MARILYN MONROE. This was her final photograph, taken shortly before her mysterious death August 5, 1962.

Photo courtesy of George Barris

deep friendship which led to the dramatic materialization of Marilyn's spirit many years later.

Marilyn's third marriage was to America's best loved baseball player, Joe DiMaggio, but this union ended in divorce as did her marriage to playwright Arthur Miller. By 1961, rumors of an affair between Marilyn and President Kennedy were surfacing and soon it was being whispered that she was also romantically involved with Robert Kennedy as well.

Throughout all this, Marilyn was growing more and more troubled. Her endless subconscious search for a father figure, her inability to bear children and the pressures of constantly living in the limelight deepened her depression. She suffered from terrible bouts of insomnia which led her to become dependent on sleeping pills and alcohol. Although she was under the care of a physician, she attempted suicide at least twice.

In June of 1962, Marilyn's perpetual tardiness and unreliability caused her to be fired by Twentieth Century-Fox. She went into seclusion in her partially furnished new home in Brentwood and stayed in touch with her friends primarily by telephone. On the last day of her life, she talked to many people, including Marlon Brando, Joe DiMaggio's son, her psychiatrist, and her housekeeper.

That evening, Marilyn made her last known phone call, to a journalist friend, Sidney Skolsky. In a slurred voice, she said she might go to Peter Lawford's beach party the next day. Her nude body was found beneath the sheet on her bed a few hours later. The phone was still clutched in her hand.

An autopsy revealed Marilyn's blood contained ten times the safe amount of phenobarbital and 20 times the recommended dosage of chloral hydrate.

How this massive overdose occurred is a question that has never been satisfactorily answered. Was it accidental? Was it suicide? Or was it murder?

Conspiracy theories quickly spread. Each and every theory began with the Monroe-Kennedy connection. The wildest conjecture was that the Kennedys themselves had killed Marilyn to keep her from going public about their sexual relationships with her. Many believed Marilyn's death was an organized crime hit meant to frame and discredit Robert Kennedy, who, as Attorney General, was fighting the Mafia and the crime-controlled Teamster's Union.

Other suspects included the FBI, and the CIA, as well as both right- and left- wing extremists. Though none of these contradictory conspiracy theories could be proven, there were enough strange things that happened during Marilyn's final night to make them seem plausible.

Robert Kennedy was probably at the Lawford's home, having flown down from San Francisco in a helicopter. That helicopter was seen landing there that day and taking off again in the morning. He or Lawford may have received a desperate call from Marilyn when she realized she was dying. They may have rushed to her house in alarm, reaching her while she was still alive.

According to statements made by two ambulance drivers, they were called to take Marilyn from her residence to the Santa Monica hospital. After this rescue attempt failed to save her life, they transported her body back to her home. Years later, Lawford would admit he sent a private investigator to search the house for a suicide note or anything incriminating she may have written.

Oddly, the police did not arrive on the scene

until five or six hours after the probable time of Marilyn's death. By then the house had been thoroughly cleaned by her housekeeper. It is likely that evidence was removed from the premises, but what that evidence might be, no one knows.

Marilyn Monroe's death was grieved by her friends and lovers alike. One of those who missed her most was her close friend, Robert Slatzer. Shortly after Marilyn's demise, Slatzer entered his home to discover the living room filled with the funereal scent of roses though there was not a flower in the house. This inexplicable phenomenon recurred periodically throughout the next decade.

In 1973, as the eleventh anniversary of Marilyn's passing drew near, Slatzer met a Hollywood psychic, Anton La Vey, at a dinner party. When La Vey learned that Slatzer had known Marilyn Monroe, he grew very excited. He explained that every 11 years, an astrological cycle which he called "the dark of moon" repeated itself. This was due to happen again on August 5, 1973 just as it had on August 5 1962 —the day Marilyn died. La Vey said he felt sure that if he were accompanied by someone who had known her, he could manifest her spirit that on night.

Surely, Slatzer was more than a little skeptical, but, thinking of the mysterious rose scent, he agreed to take part in an attempt to contact Marilyn. La Vey gained permission from the new owners of Marilyn's former home to park his car in the cul-de-sac in front of the locked gate on the night of August 5th.

At 11:45 p.m., La Vey, his wife, and Slatzer drove in and positioned the car so it faced the street. La Vey, sitting behind the steering wheel, set a small tape recorder on the dashboard. At very low volume, he began playing songs from Marilyn's films. As the themes from *Some Like It Hot*, *Gentlemen Prefer Blondes*, and *River of No Return* drifted lightly into the night, La Vey softly chanted a mantra which Slatzer did not recognize. To him, it sounded like La Vey was speaking in tongues.

The night was perfectly still. Not a leaf nor a palm frond stirred in the darkness. At 12:15 a.m., a single eucalyptus standing at the corner of the house thrashed wildly as if seized by a violent wind. For a full three minutes, the tree slapped back and forth. Then, as quickly as it had come, the thrashing was gone. The night had become quiet again. On the other side of the dimly lit street, Marilyn Monroe walked out of the shadows.

Goosebumps spread over Slatzer's body. Marilyn's blonde hair was carefully brushed, she wore white slacks, a black on white splash pattern blouse, and white loafers. Slatzer remembered that white was her favorite color.

As he and the La Veys watched breathlessly through the windshield, Marilyn slowly crossed the street and stopped not far from the car. She appeared bewildered as though she wanted to go to the gate but didn't wish to pass the automobile. After a moment's hesitation, she turned and walked off down the street.

"I'm going to follow her," Slatzer whispered. He slipped out of the car. Padding along as quietly as possible, he closed the distance between himself and the ghostly figure. Marilyn must have sensed someone was coming up behind her, because she stopped and turned around. For a brief few seconds, she stared, expressionless, at her old friend, then she vanished.

The La Veys, carrying flashlights, joined Slatzer. They sent beams of light across the grass, into the bushes, and behind the trunks of trees. There was no one on or near the street. Marilyn Monroe had gone back to the mystic realms from which she had come, leaving Slatzer to wonder why she chose not to communicate with him.

If only she had spoken, she might have revealed the truth about her death, and, even more importantly, whether or not she had at last found happiness and peace of mind. Even a smile would have been reassuring. Instead, Marilyn Monroe's happiness remains as elusive in death as it was in life.

Other famous ghosts are sometimes able to make it quite clear without speaking that they are very comfortable as spirits. One of them is the great movie hero, John Wayne. Those who have seen him since his death say he seems mellow and relaxed, very much at ease in his new existence.

During his lifetime, John Wayne captured the American imagination like no other superstar before or since. His portrayals of rugged, fearless macho men made him the ultimate symbol of heroic manliness. As one of his early co-stars, Louise Brooks, once said, "He was not just an actor. He was the hero of all mythology miraculously brought to life."

Born in Iowa in 1907, Wayne entered life as Marion Morrison. His father was a small town pharmacist for whom young Marion made after-school deliveries. It was during this period of his adolescence that he acquired his nickname. As he made his rounds, Marion was always accompanied by a small dog named Duke. Before long, the townspeople were calling the pair "Little Duke" and "Big Duke."

The Morrisons moved to California in 1917 where Marion finished high school and attended college briefly. During his summers, he found work as a prop man at Fox Studios. Soon, due to his lean physique and handsome face, he was being hired for walk-ons and bit parts. Whenever he was given screen credit, which wasn't very often, he was billed as Duke Morrison.

In 1929, director Raul Walsh gave Duke Morrison a screen test and assigned him the starring role in a western called *The Big Trail*. Walsh also gave Morrison a new name: he dubbed him John Wayne, because it "sounded American."

The Big Trail, however, was a big flop and John Wayne was back to performing low-budget B-westerns. Throughout the next decade, John Wayne took any job offered to him. He appeared in scores of cheap melodramas and serials, and even did an embarrassing stint as a Singing Cowboy. John Wayne was 32 years old before he got his big break.

It was 1939 when Wayne's longtime friend, director John Ford, cast him as the Ringo Kid in the classic western *Stagecoach*. The movie was immensely popular, critically acclaimed, and established John Wayne as a star for the rest of his life.

During the next 37 years, Wayne starred in 82 major films, 33 of which were westerns. Though Wayne never wore a uniform except as a costume, he often played war heroes such as fighter pilots, submarine commanders, and beachstorming marines. Whether his role was a burly detective, a high rolling gambler, or a barroom brawler, he was always a man of action, always a super hero.

In spite of his countless movie gunfights, John Wayne died on screen only five times. When the time came for him to die in real life, he faced death with courage and fortitude. "My biggest fight wasn't in pictures," he said after his 1963 operation for lung cancer. In 1978, he underwent open heart surgery, and, in

1979, he had his stomach removed. He died later that year.

One of John Wayne's favorite possessions was his magnificent yacht, The Wild Goose. He had purchased the 140-foot converted World War II mine sweeper in 1964 and remodeled it luxuriously. His friends said Wayne was never happier than when he stood at the helm of The Wild Goose with the wind in his face, plowing the sea with his six-man crew.

As his death approached, John Wayne decided to sell his yacht so he could be sure it passed on to someone who would truly appreciate it and care for it properly. During his search for a buyer, Wayne held long talks with a prominent Santa Monica lawyer, Lynn Hutchins. Wayne decided Hutchins was suitable to be the new owner, particularly since the two men shared the same fundamentalist religious beliefs and far right political philosophies.

Lynn Hutchins has indeed taken good care of Wayne's yacht; the boat is now almost a floating museum. Wayne's plaques and awards still hang in the main salon, and his books still populate the library. And, every so often, John Wayne himself is there. As if he is making a brief cameo appearance in a film, he is present for a few moments, then gone.

The first time John Wayne showed up was a very startling experience for Hutchins. He was alone in the boat, sleeping in Wayne's stateroom when an uneasy feeling awakened him. The room was dark, but, as his eyes adjusted, he saw someone standing in the door of the port gangway. Hutchins sat up, swung his feet to the floor, then the figure vanished.

At the time, he was not at all sure he had seen John Wayne's ghost; the figure was tall and broad-shouldered but indistinct. The apparition's second appearance, however, removed all doubt from his mind.

Hutchins was sitting by himself in the main salon, reading a book late at night. All at once, Wayne's beer glasses hanging over the bar began to shake back and forth so hard Hutchins though they might shatter. He stepped quickly to the bar, and, in the mirror behind it, he saw the reflection of a big man standing near the back of the room.

The face was unmistakable —craggy and weather beaten, with a twinkle in his eye and a slight smile. "Hello, John," Hutchins said. He turned around and there was no one. When he looked back at the mirror, the face was gone.

From then on, Hutchins became very alert to everything that happened on the yacht. Often, as he lay in bed, he heard heavy footsteps trodding up and down the deck above his stateroom. When he discussed this with Bert Minshall, the yacht's former captain, Minshall nodded knowingly. "Yep, that's the Duke all right," he said. "He had a habit of walkin' 20 laps around the deck at night before he turned in."

Others who were on board after dark, such as guests, crew members and caterers, also began catching fleeting glimpses of a tall man usually wearing a cowboy hat, a western outfit, and a loose bandanna. Hutchins became so fascinated by these repeated sightings that, in 1983, he invited a team of well-known parapsychologists to come aboard the boat to try to communicate with the spirit.

The group was headed by Patricia Hayes, a psychic who operates a training school for psychics in Atlanta, Georgia. Hayes was accompanied by three associates, William Clema, Janice Hayes and Ester-Elke Kaplan, along with Dr. William Roll, head of the

Psychical Research Foundation of Chapel Hill, North Carolina.

The five psychics held a séance in the main salon of The Wild Goose. They all agreed a contact was made with the ghostly entity but most of the information that came through was nebulous and imprecise. However, one distinct message was received by the medium, Patricia Hayes: "Tell Lady I love her."

This, as all of John Wayne's close friends know, was a direct reference to Pat Stacey, a woman with whom Wayne had a long-standing personal relationship. Wayne had always affectionately called her "Lady."

Patricia Hayes summed up the séance by saying, "What I found was he's on the boat because it's still one of his favorite places to be. He's not always here, but when he has some time available, he goes to the boat."

Lynn Hutchins concurred. "I may be the owner of The Wild Goose but it's still John's boat."

It seems to be the same with all of Hollywood's ghosts. They may be somewhere else most of the time, but, upon occasion, they get an urge to return to familiar places. Once in a while during these visitations, they are accidentally observed by those nearby. Who knows how many other famous stars come and go unseen.

How to Visit Hollywood's Haunted Houses

A driving tour of Beverly Hills can take you past several ghostly mansions. Falcon Lair, located at 1436 Bella Drive, is reached by turning off Sunset Boulevard at Benedict. Clifton Webb's house, which was remodeled in 1982, is situated at 1005 North Rexford Drive south of Wilshire Boulevard. Buster Keaton's ghost still resides at 1018 Pamela Drive while the haunted home of Jean Harlow stands quietly at 1353 Clubview Drive. Marilyn Monroe spent the final night of her life in her Helena Drive mansion just north of Wilshire.

All of these homes have gates or sensor-alarms systems and are not open to the public but can be viewed from the street.

Bibliography - Chapter 4

Eyles, Allen. **John Wayne**. New York. A.S.
       Barnes and Co. 1979.

Katz, Ephrain. **The Film Encyclopedia**. New York.
       Perigree Books. 1979.

McDonald, Archie P. **Shooting Stars**. Indianapolis.
       Indiana University Press. 1987.

Monaco, James. **The Encyclopedia of Film**.
       New York. Perigree Books. 1991.

Myers, Arthur. **The Ghostly Register**. Chicago.
       Contemporary Books, Inc. 1986.

Roberts, Nancy. **Haunted Houses: Tales From 30
       American Homes**. Chester, Connecticut.
       The Globe Pequot Press. 1988.

Steinem, Gloria. **Marilyn**. New York. Henry Holt
       & Company. 1986.

5

Reincarnation
in Hollywood

"When our bodies 'die,' it's really just that the houses for our souls don't work anymore," actress Shirley MacLaine once wrote. "We are souls who only temporarily reside in our bodies. We pass over to the astral dimension where we remain until we decide to reincarnate again. Our souls —the real us— never die. They are eternal."

Shirley MacLaine is indisputably today's most famous proponent of the ancient concept of reincarnation; she has done more than anyone else to raise contemporary awareness of the possibility of life after death. Her bestselling books describe in fascinating detail her own search for and discovery of her previous existences. MacLaine's quest took her from India to Peru, from California to New Mexico, where she sought out the trance mediums who could connect her with spiritual guides on "the other side."

From these entities, she learned she had lived many previous lives. MacLaine is convinced she was once a court jester for Louis XV and was a prostitute in still another life. She believes it is no coincidence that she has been drawn so often to hooker roles in her films.

The great actress has also discovered that she has lived as both women and men and is quite sure her daughter, Sachi, was her sister at one time. Both MacLaine and her Russian lover, Vassily Medvedjat-nikov, have no doubt that they loved one another in more than one previous lifetime.

The spiritual guides who bring Shirley information and images from the past are also often able to see the future with uncanny accuracy.

In 1981, one of her guides, a man who called himself McPherson, spoke to her through a medium known as J.Z. to tell her she would soon receive "a very fine script about a mother and daughter relation-ship and the opening shot will be that of a child's clown." McPherson predicted the film would be highly acclaimed and "you will win one of those golden stat-ues for your portrayal."

Two weeks later, Shirley MacLaine's agent hand-ed her the script for *Terms of Endearment*. MacLaine is far from being the only movie star to claim to have been reincarnated. Many others have also risked their credibility to do the same. Sylvester Stallone, though he has written no books on the subject, likes to tell his friends about the time he underwent regressive hypnosis and was able to recount a life lived during the French Revolution.

This life, he said, ended with his being guil-lotined by the Jacobins. When friends winced at the thought of being beheaded, he quickly reassured them: "Oh, no, it doesn't hurt. You don't feel anything except your head hitting the basket."

Stallone also wonders if he may have lived a life as an American Indian since, by instinct, he says he can perform Native American dances. Not surprisingly, he hopes to be reincarnated as a heavyweight boxing champion.

Other stars sometimes recall much more painful deaths. French actress and singer Juliette Greco, for example, remembers having been burned at the stake for practicing witchcraft.

Greco, best known by American film audiences for *The Sun Also Rises* and *Roots of Heaven*, has always possessed considerable psychic ability. She has the gift of precognition, enabling her to know who is knocking before the door is opened and who is calling before the telephone is answered. Greco believes these powers have carried over from a life she lived 400 years ago as a sorceress.

There are many paths one can take to enter the past. Channeling spiritual beings through an earthy medium is a favorite among those who are very serious in their searching. Regressive hypnosis can be immensely effective also, particularly since the memories come directly from the source and not a third party.

Acupuncture is also quite useful in past life recall. It is said that gold or silver needles placed in the body's "energy meridian points" and gently twirled can stimulate the memory of past lives.

One time, during a psychic therapy session with New Mexico acupuncturist Chris Griscom, Shirley MacLaine saw scenes from her life as a nomadic Mongolian girl of sixteen. So real were these images that MacLaine could vividly describe her family's huge tent with its thick rugs, tanned animal hides, and multi-colored pillows. She saw herself dining on roast camel meat and chunks of bread dipped in fermented milk. Later, she re-experienced her own brutal murder in the desert.

Many mediums use variations of techniques of spirit communication evolved in the 1930s and 1940s by the world famous psychic Edgar Cayce. By interpreting a record of a subject's life and personality along with the person's astrological aspects, Cayce was able to give past-life readings of the subject's earlier incarnations. Edgar Cayce was even able to determine that he himself was once an Egyptian high priest named Ra Ta. By employing Cayce's methods, scores of contemporary "immortality consultants" offer to trace an individual's entire "time track", sometimes as far back as Atlantis. These psychic explorations often result in astonishing findings.

One such reincarnationist, Patricia Rochelle-Diegel, has conducted nearly 50,000 past-life readings over a period of 30 years, many of which were done in the "transmigrations" of movie stars. After entering a slightly altered state of consciousness, Rochelle-Diegel is capable of revealing one or more of a person's prior lives.

For instance, upon doing a reading for William Holden, she discovered he had previously been Dr. David Livingston, who explored Africa in the Nineteenth Century. This, she believes, explained Holden's strong concern for the conservation of African wildlife.

Another past-life researcher, Ry Redd, has taken Cayce's techniques even a step further. By combining the essence of Cayce's techniques with astrology and ancient Hindu traditions of reincarnation, Redd has

GLENN FORD. Through hypnosis and historical research, this popular actor verified his five previous lives and violent deaths.

Popperphoto Limited.

been able to build up a computerized database which he believes enables him to obtain accurate past-life profiles on nearly everyone.

His readings led him to conclude that Gary Cooper was once a seafaring Spanish explorer, Clark Gable was a magician in the court of a medieval king and James Stewart lived at least one life as a pre-Columbian Native American.

Can such assumptions actually be true? Or are they mere speculation and wishful thinking? Where is the proof? the skeptics ask. What reason is there to believe in reincarnation?

Out of all the Hollywood stars who are absolutely sure to their own satisfaction that their present sojourn on this earth is not their first, there is perhaps only one who has come closest to proving it. Actor Glenn Ford not only knows he has lived five different lives over the past fifteen hundred years, but claims he can verify every one of them.

Interestingly, two of his lives revolved around Ford's own intense love of horses.

Ford was born into his present life in 1916, 31 years after his last death. He grew up in Glanford, Quebec, under the name Gwyllyn Samuel Newton Ford. In 1923, he moved with his family to Santa Monica, California, where he attended high school and rode his first horse at the age of ten. Ford became so adept at handling horses that, when he became a teenager, he caught the attention of Will Rogers, who gave him a part-time job exercising his polo ponies.

Ford was also developing an interest in acting. He appeared in high school plays, West Coast stage shows, and, by 1939, was landing small parts in movies. In 1942, he starred along side Rita Hayworth in a sultry film called *Gilda* and with Bette Davis in *A*

Stolen Life. By 1958, a Motion Picture Herald poll found him to be the "number one box office star in America."

Although Glenn Ford played a wide variety of roles, ranging from school teachers to naval officers, he was always at his best in westerns, in which he invariably did his own stunt riding.

At one point in the 1960s, Ford read *Psychic*, the autobiography of the famous clairvoyant Peter Hurkos. The actor was so fascinated by Hurkos' incredible paranormal talent that they arranged to meet and hold a hypnotic session in California.

The hypnotist was Dr. Harley Alexander, chief of staff of Santa Monica Hospital. The doctor put Hurkos under a hypnotic trance and told him only "I am a surgeon. I operated this morning." Hurkos, to the astonishment of everyone present, then proceeded to describe the entire operation in exact and accurate detail.

Ford was so impressed that he immediately began studying hypnosis. After reading Morey Bernstein's book *The Search for Bridey Murphy*, Ford eagerly underwent regressive hypnosis himself. The tape recordings of these sessions were even more remarkable than Bernstein's incredible Bridey Murphy tapes.

The hypnotist Ford chose was an eminent one, Dr. Maurice Benjamin, a psychologist at the University of Southern California at Los Angeles. Benjamin put Ford into a peaceful trance and said, "Let's go back to another life, another time. Tell me what you are experiencing."

"Ahh, bread," Ford said, in a gruff cowboy voice he had never used in a film. "Bread and coffee. All we ate. That's all we ate. I'm full."

"Where are you?"

"Cheyenne. It's hot. Dust everywhere. I want to buy some buttermilk."

"What is the date?"

"1880."

"What is your name?"

"I'm Charlie. Charlie Hill. I work for Mister Charlie Goodnight. I'm his trail boss. I take care of his cattle."

Charlie Hill went on to talk about his life and death. He'd ridden his first horse at age six and spent most of his life in the saddle. He had worked his way up from young "drag rider" to "side rider," then on to "high boy", then "trail boss." Mr. Goodnight paid him five dollars a month, and on payday in Cheyenne, "you could have a pretty girl for fifty cents in a fancy, fancy house."

Charlie Hill died in an ambush. "I didn't expect it. I trusted somebody I shouldn't have trusted. I wasn't hit be the first shot, you know. Well, he hit me in the back of the head and my neck. He kept shooting and I wanted to die fast."

"What did you experience as your life was passing?"

"I didn't want my horse to get hurt. He didn't have to shoot my horse."

Charlie Hill had died a dramatic, almost cinematic death. But had he been a real person? Or was he merely a product of Glenn Ford's subconscious imagination?

It wasn't difficult to learn that there really was a Charles Goodnight —he was a famed cattleman in his day— but it took a trip to Colorado by two researchers from the University of California to discover archival proof that there actually had been a

Charlie Hill and that he was killed in 1885.

Next, Ford was to learn that 40 years before his death as a cowboy, he had lived as a Scottish piano teacher named Charles Stuart. He was a bachelor who gave lessons to little children whom he referred to as "a bunch of fibberti-gibbets. That's all they are. They don't care. They don't want to learn. They're just fibberti-gibbets." Stuart died of consumption (pulmonary tuberculosis) in 1840 at the age of 38 and was buried in Elgin, Scotland.

During a hypnotic session at UCLA, Ford, representing Chrales Stuart, played the piano skillfully. Afterwards, he admitted with a chuckle, "I can't play a note."

Later, when researchers in Scotland located and photographed a Charles Stuart's tombstone dated 1802-1840 in an old Elgin cemetery, Ford was stunned. "That really shook me up," he said.

"I felt immediately that it was the place where I was buried."

Prior to his life as a piano player, Ford lived a considerably more exciting life. Born in 1680 as Emile Launvaux, he was a member of the Royal Cavalry of King Louis XIV at the Palace of Versailles. From the age of 16, Launvaux reveled in the pomp and pageantry of the Middle Ages.

"Are you handsome?" the hypnotist asked.

Launvaux laughed good naturedly. "Oh, no gentleman says he's handsome. That's up to someone else to say."

"Do you have any girlfriends?"

"I've dallied with all of the ladies of the court," Launvaux answered proudly. "That's how I got in trouble. I was very indiscreet with a lady ... I died young."

"How old were you?"

"Twenty. No, 23. I had to duel the court swordsman. You duel with the best swordsman in the court and he's going to kill you. But if you are a gentleman, you accept that. He kissed me with his rapier and then he hit my chest."

The hypnotized Ford touched himself below the ribcage. "It went right through me...uh...hurt. But the girl... the girl was worth it."

Throughout this session, Glenn Ford spoke 18th Century French with ease, something he cannot do in his present incarnation. After the session ended, he opened his shirt to reveal a small birthmark in his chest at the exact place where he had pointed.

The actor continued to move further and further back. He relived experiences from a life as a British sailor in the 1660s. Though the young seaman had been forced or "pressed" to serve aboard a merchant ship, he soon found he loved being at sea. "I like the smell of the wood," he said. "And I like the smell of the sea. I like not knowing where I'm going."

Upon his return to London from the East Indies during the year that the "Thames froze over," he found thousands dying of bubonic plague. He became one of them. "It was terrible, y'know. We couldn't avoid it. We had no one to tell us what to do." At the age of "20 candles," the young fellow perished in agony.

No details from this lifetime could be corroborated, nor could any from his original incarnation as a Third Century Christian, 1,300 years earlier. This time around, Ford was Flavius, a lowly citizen of Rome who was thrown to a lion in the Colesium for refusing to renounce his belief in Christianity.

"What was it like?" the hypnotist asked.

"He killed me quick. I wanted it to happen quick. I must have been good, honorable ... because the lion was kind to me and did it very quick."

From Christian martyr to plague victim, from sword-pierced duelist to consumptive pianist, and from bushwhacked cowboy to world-renowned movie star, Glenn Ford has lived —and relived— enough excitement for at least six men. After more than 200 years of life on earth and nearly 1,500 years on the astral plane, there is undoubtedly very little he has not experienced.

Gone is his fear of death and strong is his belief that "the thing most needed by the human race is a renewal of faith in its own immortality."

Bibliography - Chapter 5

Boar. Roger and Blundell, Nigel. **Mystery, Intrigue, and The supernatural**. New York. Dorset Press. 1987.

Cranston, Sylvia and Williams, Carey. **Reincarnation: A New Horizon in Science, Religion,and Society**. New York. Julian Press. 1984.

Hansen-Steiger, Sherry and Steiger, Brad. **Hollywood and the Supernatural**. New York. St. Martin's Press. 1990.

Lee, John. *Time Magazine*. Los Angeles. Time, Inc. September 10, 1984.

MacLaine, Shirley. **Dancing in the Light**. New York, Bantam Books. 1985.

Smith, Susy. **Reincarnation for the Millions**. New York. Dell Publishing Company. 1969.

6

Dastardly Deeds in Old San Francisco

Early San Francisco was a high-roller's dream town. In the wake of the California Gold Rush, the tiny port city had grown from 850 residents to 25,000 in just three years. Wealth from the gold fields poured into town along with people of every nationality and walk of life.

The unpaved, usually muddy streets teemed with humanity. Oregonians and Missourians, New Yorkers and Texans rubbed elbows with native-born Mexican *Californios*, adventurous Australians and a steadily growing number of Chinese. As diverse as these people were, they all had one thing in common: every one of them planned to get rich quick. And there were plenty of ways to make a lot of money in the wild, frenzied boomtown of San Francisco in 1851.

Property owners who had purchased prime bay

81

area land in 1848 at $16 an acre were now selling their lots to the newly rich "Fortyniners" for $3,000 a piece. Merchants reaped bonanzas selling scarce goods at outrageous prices. A pound of hard bread went for $2; a pound of cheese could run as high as $3.

Prices were astronomical, but so were wages. Bricklayers and stone masons made an unheard of 20 dollars per day, and even laundresses' sweaty labor brought them between $6 and $8 daily.

Honest work and legal business transactions were well-rewarded in early San Francisco but, as could be expected, the most lucrative enterprises were criminal ones. Hundreds of the West Coast's most rapacious and talented criminals swarmed into San Francisco like hungry foxes in a very crowded henhouse.

From two-bit grifters and light-fingered pickpockets to skilled, professional gamblers and silver-tongued con men, the town teemed with sly scoundrels. And each one knew that the expression "gold is where you find it" did not mean they had to head off into the hills with a pick and a shovel to make a fortune. The slick gamblers all knew the truth of the old saying "a fool and his money are soon parted," and every scheming swindler agreed with P.T Barnum's adage that "there's a sucker born every minute."

One of the most common scams was the one used to fleece newly-arrived gold seekers. When the eager but naive immigrants disembarked from the tall ships that had brought them to California, they were often welcomed by respectable-looking, smooth-talking men offering transportation to the gold fields. For a fee, these savvy fellows promised not only a place in a wagon but tents, tools, machines for washing gold, and ample food as well.

To greenhorns, confused and bewildered by the bustling city, the proposition was irresistible. Once they had trustingly handed over their money, their new-found "friends" hurried away to "make the necessary arrangements" and, of course, were never seen again.

Capers of this sort were common, quick, and easy, but they netted only paltry sums of money. The real con men, the big-time grifters, were quite contemptuous of this type of petty theft. They set their sights much, much higher.

Some of America's most creative and ingenious con artists plied their trades in San Francisco in the wild, free-wheeling 1850s. Two of the boldest were "General" John Wilson and his partner, John A. Collins. Together, they pulled off the biggest sting of the gold rush era, making themselves the most hated, envied —and begrudgingly admired— swindlers of their time.

The story of this skillfully masterminded hoax began on a foggy January morning in 1851 when a small coastal vessel named the *Chesapeake* pulled into San Francisco Bay. The *Chesapeake* was a delivery boat of modest size which made regular runs between Oregon and San Francisco carrying mail, cargo, and passengers. Uncharacteristically, it was two days late.

The first two passengers to come ashore were Wilson and Collins, who strode brusquely through the crowds and went at once to an assayer's office. From there, they hurried to a nearby law firm. The next morning, they set up a meeting with several of San Francisco's leading bankers.

When everyone had gathered in the private office of the president of the Crocker-Woolworth Central Bank, John Wilson closed the door and said, "Gentlemen, not one word of what Mr. Collins and I plan to discuss with you here today is to be mentioned outside of his room. Is that understood?" The bankers, who were not accustomed to being addressed in that manner, glanced at one another. They all frowned, but they all nodded.

John Wilson was an imposing man. He claimed to be a former U.S. Army general, and there was certainly an intimidating air of authority about him. While the others sat in chairs, he remained standing; he paced the room with his shoulders squared, and his hands clasped behind his back as he spoke.

"Last week," he began, "Mr. Collins and I sailed down the coast from Portland to explore investment opportunities in San Francisco. On our third night, an unfortunate accident occurred. Somehow, a large pipe wrench fell into the engine compartment of the *Chesapeake*, jammed the cog-wheels and caused extensive damage.

"While repairs were being made, Collins and I asked to be taken ashore so that we could hike the beach and exercise our legs. Imagine our surprise when we discovered the beach was a long strand of black sand fairly glittering with golden specks.

"Gold, gentlemen, in sand so rich you can scoop up a fortune with your bare hands. We brought back samples and had them assayed yesterday. Mr. Collins will pass the report around. As you can see, the beach can be expected to yield $10 per pound of sand.

"We have dispatched two eminent mineralogists to the site to determine its full potential. We should receive word of their findings within a few days. In the meantime, Collins and I are taking the necessary steps to form a mining company. Once we have professional confirmation of the true value of our discovery, we will begin selling shares in our corporation.

"For the time being, the location of the gold field cannot be revealed. I'm sure all of you remember what happened when word of John Sutter's strike got out in 1849. Thousands of people descended on Sutter's Mill and helped themselves. That, I can assure you, is not going to happen this time. No one except bona fide investors will be allowed to set foot on the Pacific Mining Company's property."

General Wilson and John Collins shook hands all around and went on their way, leaving the awed bankers to ponder the incredible news they had so unexpectedly been given. The two con men let a suspenseful week go by before they set up a second meeting at the Central Bank. This time, they passed around three letters that they said had been mailed to them from Trinity County in northern California. The first letter began:

Mr. John A. Collins
Secretary, Pacific Mining Company.
Dear Sir,
As you wished, I am writing you about all I have seen of the deposit of gold on the beach you discovered ...the black sand runs for the entire length of the shoreline. At six to 12 inches below the surface, the concentration of gold is even higher. It is difficult to conceive how enough men could be found to exhaust this resource in one entire generation.
Yours respectfully,
M.C. Thompson

The second letter verified the first:
I fully concur in the statements made by Mr.

*Thompson. Having been with him at the time men-
tioned, I have no hesitation in saying that he has
not in one particular deviated from the facts in
regard to this matter.*
    C.W. Kinsey

Both letters were notarized, and the third docu-
ment was signed by Trinity County Justice of the
Peace, L.B. Gilkey, who attested that he had personally taken the statements from the two mineralogists
and put them on legal record.

"Gentlemen," said General Wilson, "the Pacific
Mining Company is now ready to begin selling
shares."

And sell them they did. All of San Francisco's
banks invested heavily and, after an ecstatic article
extolling the the "Fabulous New Find of Immensely
Rich Gold Ore" appeared in the *Alta California*,
scores of eager, monied men lined up in front of the
pair's offices on Market Street to invest. The two
entrepreneurs sold shares as quickly as they could be
printed, and stashed all the money in a large safe, the
combination of which was known only to them.

Next, the Pacific Mining Company engaged a
large clipper schooner, *The Empire*, and outfitted it
with mining tools, a sand washer, and other necessary
supplies. "The time has come to announce the location of the Golden Strand," Wilson told his sharehold-
ers. "Tomorrow, all of you will sail forth to a glorious
beach extending from Trinidad Bay to the Kalamath
River. In less than a week, you will set foot on the new
El Dorado. I promise you it will be the most unforget-
table day of your lives."

In the morning, the fog had barely lifted from
the Buena Cove of San Francisco Bay when *The*

Empire, packed to capacity with excited, jubilant would-be gold miners, headed north along the coast. Collins and Wilson stood on deck amid a cheering crowd of well-wishers, waving their derby hats until the schooner's sails neared the horizon. Then, they strode rapidly uphill to their offices, locked the doors, pulled down the shades, and began turning the dial on the safe.

A mere week and a half later, to everyone's surprise, the Empire returned to San Francisco. An angry horde of cursing men stormed ashore shouting, "We've been flim-flammed! The Golden Strand is a fraud! There's no gold! Not a single speck!"

Howling with rage, the mob descended on the Pacific Mining Company, where, of course, they found the offices deserted, the safe open and empty. Wilson and Collins were long gone. No one had seen them leave town, but a liveryman remembered renting them a fast horse and a hansom cab the day after *The Empire* set sail.

It was now painfully obvious to everyone that all it had taken to make fools of them were a few sacks of salted assay samples and three forged letters.

Just how much money the investors lost is unknown but it was easily well over a million dollars. No one knows what became of Wilson and Collins, though unconfirmable rumors placed them somewhere in South America living a life of luxury.

San Francisco continued to grow rapidly, doubling in size every decade. The rip-roaring Gold Rush Days soon ended. Gone were the long rows of gleaming, lantern-lit gambling tents and the makeshift canvas houses where the harlots of Portsmouth Square entertained their clients. In their place stood ornate casinos, grandiose hotels, fancy opera houses and sumptuous restaurants. Trolley cars clanged past the solid stone banks lining Market Street while telegraph poles as tall as the masts of the ships in the harbor climbed the hills.

The "City by the Bay" became very cosmopolitan, and its financial institutions grew quite sophisticated. Consequently, San Francisco's wily criminal element had to become much more ingenious and creative in its schemes. Two good examples of the new breed of grifters were a couple of roving con men named Charles Becker and Frank Dean. This slick duo had perfected a very smooth "paper hanging" scam which they repeated in city after city across the land. In the fall of 1895, they brought their act to San Francisco.

Frank Dean was the first to arrive in town. He rented a furnished office in the Chronicle Building and had the words "F.H. Dean, Stockbroker" painted on the frosted-glass door. Next, he opened a modest $1,000 checking account at San Francisco's Nevada Bank. The following day, Dean traveled by rail to the small town of Woodland, near Sacramento. There he made a deposit of similar size at the local bank under the name of Arthur Holmes.

Upon his return to San Francisco, Dean wrote a $100 check to himself on his Bank of Woodland account, signed it Arthur Holmes and cashed it at the Nevada Bank. Over the next few weeks he wrote several more checks to himself, from one name and account to the other. In short order, Frank Dean established himself as a steady and reliable bank customer.

In early December, he made a second trip to Woodland where he obtained a certified check for $22 payable to Frank Dean. Now, Charles Becker, came on the scene. Becker, a dapper fellow with intense eyes and a well-groomed mustache, was what was then called a "scratch" —a master forger. He met Dean in his San Francisco hotel room and carefully examined the check. "It'll be a piece of cake, Frank," he said with a smile.

Becker opened the satchel in which he carried the tools of his trade: small bottles of colored inks, bleaches, erasers, and an assortment of steel tipped pens, small sharp knives and soft brushes. Dean, knowing his partner would need complete solitude, said, "I'm going down to the bar for a brandy. I'll see you later."

Becker hardly noticed Dean's departure; he was already studying the check with a magnifying glass. The sum of 22 dollars appeared four times. Opposite Frank Dean's name $22.00 had been penned in. On the line below, "twenty two & .00" was handwritten and was followed by a long dash. In each upper corner, $22.00 had been perforated into the paper.

Without hesitation, Becker selected exactly the right pen and shade of ink. After practicing a few times on a piece of scratch paper, he added an additional zero to the $22.00 and turned the period into a comma. Next, with a steady, skillful hand, he used a thin-tipped brush and a mild bleach solution to gently remove the "& .00" and the dash without damaging the paper. After again practicing on a scratch pad, he wrote in the word "thousand" with the same signature on the original check.

Now, he turned his attention to the perforations. Carefully, he punched in an extra zero at the end of each "22.00" and changed the period to a comma. This completed the work. The check had been "raised" and Charles Becker was also ready for a brandy.

When the Nevada Bank opened the next morning, Frank Dean brought in the check and deposited it into his account. Twenty four hours later he returned and filled out a withdrawal slip for $22,000. The cashier counted out the money, and Dean put it in his briefcase and strolled out the door. The swindle went undiscovered for several days, giving Becker and Dean plenty of time to put California far behind them. No doubt they thought they had made a perfect getaway and would never be apprehended. That might well have been true had it not been for a very remarkable police officer, San Francisco's Captain of Detectives, Isaiah Wrigley Lees.

Lees was a San Francisco legend. His distinguished law enforcement career spanned four decades beginning in 1854 when he walked a beat as a street cop in some of the roughest, toughest parts of town. Big and burly, honest and fearless, young Isaiah helped tame the Barbary Coast. In 1860 we was promoted to detective and soon became well-known for his ability to solve the city's most difficult crimes. Over the years, Isaiah Lees arrested multitudes of thieves and murderers, bank robbers and stick up men, and was especially adept at cracking cases of embezzlement, counterfeiting, and electoral fraud. He was, as the *San Francisco Chronicle* once wrote, "the greatest criminal catcher the West has ever known."

By 1895, Lees' hair and beard were white with age, but his mind was as keen and sharp as ever. When John Kavanaugh, president of the Nevada Bank, brought him news of the Becker and Dean caper, Lees' eyes sparkled with interest.

"I don't suppose you've got much chance of catching those birds," Kavanaugh fumed. "They've flown the coop and could be anywhere in the country by now."

"That's certainly true," Lees admitted. "But the long arm of the law reaches a lot further now-a-days than it used to. Give me a little time to work on this, John. I just might come up with a surprise for you."

Captain Lees called in two of his best detectives. "I want you to talk to everyone who ever laid eyes on Frank Dean while he was in San Francisco," he told them. "Interview the tellers and cashiers at the bank. Find out which hotel he stayed in. Question the desk clerks, the bellhops, the elevator operators and the bartenders. I want a completely detailed description of this plucky rogue who calls himself Frank Dean."

It was nearly dark when the detectives returned to Lees' office. They flipped open their notebooks and began reading the information they had collected: "He's forty-ish. Tall. About five-ten. Probably 170 pounds. Dark eyes. Narrow Nose. Brown hair, parted in the middle. No sideburns. Protruding ears. Clean shaven, and —get this, boss— a small, thin scar on his chin."

"Well done, boys," Lees said. He drew out his watch. "It's getting late. Leave your notes with me and go home to your families. I'm going to stay here a while. I think it's time to take a little trip through my Rogue's Gallery."

Isaiah Lees was a man ahead of his time. He was constantly coming up with new investigative techniques and was the first detective in the United States to make use of what would become known as "mug shots." For years, Lees had made sure every criminal arrested in San Francisco was photographed, whether he or she wanted to be or not. The photos were kept in what grew to be an enormous file which Lees called his Rogue's Gallery.

By the late 1880s, many other police departments around the country were building similar collections of grainy, black and white portraits. As communications between cities improved, they began exchanging photographs to aid each other in their investigations.

As night fell over San Francisco, Lees ambled down the hallway to the room where the files were stored. He turned up the gas light, pulled out the drawer labeled "Forgers" and started thumbing through the folders, one by one. It was nearly midnight when he lifted up a single photograph, smiled triumphantly at it and said, "Well, how do you do, Mr. Dean."

When the detectives reported for work in the morning, Lees handed them the picture. "Here's our man, boys," he said. "He was caught five years ago trying to cash a raised check. Called himself Harry Webster in those days. Got out on bail and skipped town. A slick fellow, all right, but a clumsy forger. Now, however, it appears he has teamed up with someone who is a very, very good scratch.

"I want you to show this photo to everyone you talked to yesterday. Once we get a positive identification, I'll locate the negative, get copies made, and mail them to the police departments of all the major cities in the country with a request that they be distributed to local banks. Then, we'll just sit back and wait."

Surprisingly, Lees did not have to wait long. A few weeks later, an alert Minneapolis bank teller who had posted one of the photos near his teller window spotted Frank Dean standing in line, waiting to open an account. Dean was arrested, and his hotel room was put under surveillance. When Charles Becker showed up at the room with his satchel in hand, he, too, was apprehended. Both men were extradited back to San Francisco where they were tried, convicted, and sentenced to eight years apiece. That gave them plenty of time to stare out through the bars of their cells and marvel at how easily an old California police captain had brought about their downfall from nearly 2,000 miles away.

Isaiah Lees was unquestionably a truly great crime fighter. His tireless, lifetime crusade against San Francisco's lawbreakers rid the town of an enormous assortment of nefarious characters.

Bibliography - Chapter 6

Beck, Warren A. and Williams, David A. **California. A History of the Golden State**. Garden City, New York. Doubleday & Company, Inc. 1972.

Felchner, William J. *Frontier Times* magazine. Austin, Texas. Western Publication, Inc. June, 1985.

Jackson, Donald Dale. **Gold Dust**. New York. Alfred A. Knopf, Inc. 1980.

Rosenhouse, Leo. *Treasure World* magazine Garland, Texas. Treasure World Publishing Company. October-November, 1971.

Secrest, William B. *True West* magazine. Austin, Texas. Western Publications, Inc. May-June, 1976, May 1993.

7

California Duelin'

The field of honor was shrouded in early morning fog. Through the drifting mists came the forlorn cries of seagulls as an audience of spectators gathered quietly on the edge of the dewy grass. Soon, two horse-drawn carriages appeared and came to a halt across from the crowd.

From each buggy, a man wearing a long grey overcoat stepped down. Without glancing at one another, the two men walked side by side to the center of the field. They were followed by three equally somber men, two seconds and a doctor. The grim entourage stopped in the middle of the open space where the two hard-eyed men removed their overcoats, handed them to their seconds, and stretched out their arms to be patted down for concealed weapons or protective body armor.

While the hushed crowd on the sidelines strained to hear the words, one of the seconds spoke: "My best friend has been challenged to defend his honor in a duel. Under the code of chivalry, it is his right to make the choice of weapons. He has chosen pistols." The second then lifted the lid of an ornate wooden gun case, revealing two loaded Navy Colt revolvers resting on the box's green felt lining.

The duelists each selected one and turned their backs on one another. The second's voice rose a little as he spoke. "When I give the word, you will walk forward ten paces, turn and face each other. On the count of three, you will fire. Advance!"

With their revolvers at their sides, the silent men strode forward, then halted. Each then turned and planted his feet firmly. A voice yelled out. "One!" The duelists cocked and raised their pistols. "Two!" They extended their arms and aimed. "Three!" The guns roared. One man fell; the other walked away.

This was a drama that was enacted many times in early California. Between 1850 and 1860, several hundred duels were reported in the state's newspapers and it is probable that an equal number went unrecorded.

During an era when personal honor was valued above all else, no insult to a man's character could be tolerated. Anyone who felt he had been slandered, ridiculed, humiliated (or, worst of all, cuckolded) was bound to defend his reputation, even if it meant sustaining a grievous wound or even forfeiting life itself.

Duels were usually fought with pistols or rifles, but, in the spring of 1854, two Frenchmen clashed using swords, prompting the *San Francisco Daily Bulletin* to praise their daring, though non-lethal, performance because it "varied the monotony of firearms and hopefully will introduce a new fashion."

Newspaper coverage of duels helped make them one of California's most popular spectator sports. Frequently, the papers published the time and place of an upcoming duel and always allowed angry, offended men to issue their challenges in paid advertisements such as this one which appeared in the Alta California on May 1, 1852:

I hearby post and publish Edward Gilbert as a scoundrel, liar, and poltroon and declare him to be out of pale of gentlemen's society. I will meet him whenever and wherever required and face him with whatever weapons he may decide upon.

> *J.W. Denver*

Publicity of this sort always assured good attendance at a duel and guaranteed a lot of betting on the outcome. Early Californians loved to gamble. They would bet on anything from roulette wheels and horse races to boxing matches, cock fights, and duels. Undeniably, there was a special excitement about placing a wager on a duel, because it was the one competition in which men put their lives on the line.

Duels were also fascinating because no one could be sure how they would turn out. One could bet on someone who looked like a sure winner and wind up watching him land on his back. Affairs of the honor very often had surprising outcomes. In the case of the Denver-Gilbert duel, there was little doubt as to what the outcome would be, but it was a dramatic encounter nonetheless.

J.W. Denver was a State Senator for Trinity County and Edward Gilbert was the muckraking editor of the *Alta California*. During the legislative session of 1852, Gilbert wrote a scathing editorial about Denver, accused him of being an obsequious pawn of big business and a betrayer of public trust.

When the enraged senator stormed into Gilbert's office and tossed his challenge on the desk, the editor read it disinterestedly and handed it back. "Give this to my secretary on your way out," he said. "I'll run it in the next issue —if I have space for it."

"Are you man enough to meet me on the field of honor?" Denver demanded.

"Of course," Gilbert shrugged. "I'm a busy man but I'll try to work it into my schedule." After the furious Denver stomped out with a mighty door slam, the editor sagged in his chair. "Are you all right, Mr. Gilbert?" his frightened secretary asked.

Though his face was starting to twitch now, Gilbert managed a weak smile. "Yes, Ms. Cartwright," he said. "For a man who just signed his own death warrant, I feel remarkably relaxed."

Edward Gilbert knew he didn't have a chance against J.W. Denver. The senator was an expert marksman, whereas Gilbert could hardly hold a pistol. Everyone admired him for his courage but almost no one was foolish enough to bet any money on him.

On the morning of the duel, Denver and Gilbert faced off in Oak Grove near Sacramento. Their weapons were Wesson rifles; the distance was 40 paces. At the command to fire, Denver deliberately shot high, far above Gilbert's head. Gilbert fired and missed. Having given his opponent a sporting chance, Denver than re-aimed and sent the spunky little editor flying backward with bullet through his heart.

There were many similar occasions when California's duelists were badly matched. Usually, this meant the deadliest man won. But from time to time an underdog was clever enough to figure a way to offset his disadvantage, and sometimes even give himself a slight edge. Such was the case in the duel between Henry Teschemacher and Lieutenant Randall Bonneycastle in 1854.

Teschemacher was a young Sacramento haberdasher who had recently married a petite and pretty schoolteacher named Anne. Bonneycastle, a decorated U.S. Army officer, was dashingly handsome and well aware of it.

One balmy spring evening, the Teschemachers attended a grand party in Sacramento's finest hotel ballroom. After they had danced in a couple of sets, Henry went to the punchbowl to get them some refreshments. In his absence, Bonneycastle stepped up to Anne, ardently pressed her hand, and whispered an indecent proposal in her ear. The shocked young woman blushed bright red, rushed at once to her husband's side, and told him of Bonneycastle's insolence.

Livid with anger, Henry Teschemacher dashed across the room, and, in front of all the guests, gave the offender a stiff shove and shouted in his face "You filthy swine! How dare you insult my wife with your foul mouth?"

Bonneycastle, who was about to light a cigar, threw his pantela on the floor like a gauntlet. In a patronizing voice, he snapped, "And how dare you, a common shopkeeper, insult an officer and a gentleman like myself? Apologize, little man. Or back your words with deeds on the field of honor."

"I'll meet you anywhere, anytime!" Teschemacher blurted out. Soon a date was set for the duel.

The Teschemachers left the party and returned to their little apartment above Henry's store where they sat on the edge of their bed and began to tremble. Anne was near tears as she said, "Oh, Henry, you're no match for him. He's a professional soldier. Did you see all his medals?" Henry, who was starting to realize the gravity of his situation, nodded glumly.

Henry Teschemacher was too badly shaken to

sleep that night, until, near one o'clock, he got an idea. A quiver of hope flowed over him. "It just might work," he said to himself.

When the day of the duel dawned, the two men walked toward each other across a broad pasture outside of Sacramento. Lieutenant Bonneycastle, resplendent in his full dress uniform, eyed Teschemacher contemptuously. "I assume you have made your choice of weapons?" he smirked.

"Yes," Teschemacher said calmly. "I have chosen rifles. I will fire your rifle and you will fire mine."

Bonneycastle's cocky smile faded momentarily. Then he handed over his gun and accepted Teschemacher's in return. While Anne Teschemacher held her breath on the edge of the crowd, the men paced off 40 steps apiece, turned toward each other and listened to the countdown. At "Three!" they fired simultaneously .

Bonneycastle missed and Teschemacher's bullet hit the Lieutenant's hand, sending the rifle and one of his fingers spinning away.

As Bonneycastle hopped about, yelling in pain, Teschemacher handed the gun to the lieutenant's second. "My old rifle always shoots a little to the left," he admitted. "One has to practice to correct for it. I must have forgotten to tell Lieutenant What's-his-name about that."

Anne Teschemacher ran happily across the field and threw herself into her husband's arms while the exuberant spectators cheered, applauded, and waved their hats.

Many times during this excessively chivalrous era, men issued challenges on behalf of friends who had been publicly slandered or ridiculed, for an affront to a respected peer was as offensive as an insult to one's self. Perhaps the classic example of this type of death-defying loyalty was the Walker-Graham encounter in 1851.

William Walker was the editor of the *San Francisco Herald*, a very partisan tabloid which effusively praised Democrats and ruthlessly attacked Republicans. One of Walker's favorite targets was a highly respected Probate Judge named R.N. Morrison. On January 12, 1851, Walker penned an especially vitriolic piece on Morrison, calling him everything from corrupt to senile.

Morrison's six young law clerks were outraged when they read Walkers' tirade. They all had great admiration for the kindly, old jurist. To them, Morrison was a mentor, a role model, and a father figure.

"If the judge were a younger man, he would challenge Walker to a duel," said one of the clerks. "But he's too old now, too slow, and his hand is no longer steady. "

"That's true," said another. "Therefore it's up to one of us to stand in the judge's place. I propose we draw straws to see who it will be." Everyone agreed, and six bristles were broken off a broom for a drawing. The youngest of the six clerks, William Hicks Graham, drew the short straw.

The other five clerks glanced at each other, uneasily. Will Graham was a frail, awkward little man with thick glasses who couldn't have hit a fly with a swatter. "Maybe we'd better draw again," the eldest clerk suggested. "You're no match for William Walker, Will. He's already fought three duels."

"No," Graham insisted. "I have won the right to defend the judge's honor. Tonight, I will issue the challenge."

That evening, Will Graham, accompanied by the

other clerks, entered William Walker's favorite watering hole, the Oriental Saloon. Walker was standing at the bar with a glass of bourbon before him and a long, thin cheroot between his fingers. An aura of menace always seemed to hover over this lean, grey-eyed man; his gaunt face made him look more like an undertaker than a journalist.

Graham stepped up to him, and, in a voice that quavered only slightly, said, "I know you are not a gentleman but I imagine that even a low-down piece of trash like you will recognize an insult when one is offered." He picked up Walker's drink and threw it in is face.

Walker barely flinched. His eyes remained steady as he hissed, "Dawn tomorrow. The plaza at Mission Delores. Pistols." With that, he stalked out the door into the night.

Word of the impending duel spread quickly from saloon to saloon so, when dawn finally came, a fair-sized crowd had assembled beneath the sagging porticos of the crumbling old church. There was not much betting that day, because few were foolhardy enough to bet the ten-to-one odds on the brash young upstart.

Graham and Walker both arrived with the sun and walked across the hard-packed, bare dirt to the center of the plaza. Walker's second announced, "As you know, Mr. Walker has made pistols his choice of weaponry. He further demands that after each shot is fired, each contestant will take one step forward before firing again. You will both now walk ten paces apiece, turn, and await the command to begin shooting."

Walker, wearing his best black suit and his favorite satin bowtie, and Graham, shivering a little in a collarless white shirt and suspenders, walked ahead as instructed and turned.

"Fire!" the second shouted. Both guns roared and both men missed. Each took a long, deliberate step forward and discharged their pistols a second time. Graham's hat sailed away, and, to his complete amazement, he watched Walker's right leg buckle under. Graham had hit the master duelist's thigh, causing him to topple to his knees. When he could not rise enough to take his next step, Walker cried out. "Enough!"

Will Graham gawked in amazement. He could scarcely believe he had not only survived unharmed but had actually been victorious. His fellow clerks shouted a loud hurrah and ran onto the plaza to shake Will's hand. Then, they swarmed through the crowd to collect bets they had felt obligated to place but never expected to win.

Young Will was quite a hero around San Francisco after that. He went on to become a prominent lawyer and was elected District Attorney of Mono County in 1865. William Walker's fate was quite different. He was destined to hear the roar of guns again, though not on a field of his own choosing.

In 1855, he became a "filibuster." As head of a large expedition of mercenaries, he entered Nicaragua, declared himself president, and seized control of the country. When at last he was ousted, he was arrested in Honduras and promptly put up against a wall. The last word Walker heard was "Fire!"

Back in California, the state's proud duelists were continuing to respond to that same command, still blazing away in self-righteous indignation. Although most duels were dead-serious affairs, they sometimes turned out to be more like comic-opera farces. Shortly after the Graham-Walker shootout, two

State Senators, Joseph McCorkle and William M. Gwin, squared off with pistols on a grassy meadow outside San Francisco. The wild melee that took place that morning was hardly the sort of dramatic spectacle the crowds expected to see.

McCorkle and Gwin had been feuding for several weeks over a piece of proposed legislation. Their arguments had grown more heated by the day. Soon, they were shouting and cursing at each other. After an especially livid exchange of insults, the two furious politicians realized there was only one thing left for them to do: head for the field of honor.

Due to the prominence of the two men, an unusually large crowd of spectators showed up to witness this historic event. There was a festive air on the dueling ground that day; many people had brought picnic baskets and bottles of beer. There was a round of applause when the two gallant men strutted purposefully out to the center of the grassy arena.

Stoically, McCorkle and Gwin hefted up their revolvers, paced off the steps and glared at each other. At the count of three, they both fired. McCorkle's first shot knocked down a sailor standing at the front of the crowd and Gwin's bullet nicked the ear of a little newsboy who ran off bawling like a wounded calf.

Instantly, the horrified spectators began scrambling out of the way, tipping over picnic baskets and beer bottles in their panic. The duelists fired again. This time, McCorkle feiled a donkey grazing innocently at the rim of the pasture.

As the crowd edged further and further back, the senators continued to blaze away, tossing up clumps of grass and making lots of noise, but causing no further injuries. When both had emptied their pistols, they declared themselves satisfied and swaggered back to their waiting carriages. The only fatality was the unfortunate donkey, whose demise prompted the *San Francisco Bulletin* to comment that "The wrong jackass got shot." It seems quite probable that McCorkle's and Gwin's political careers were buried along with the donkey.

California's most famous duel was fought in 1859 by David S. Terry and David C. Broderick. Their confrontation resulted in a death which shocked all of California and led many people to believe the shooting was actually a carefully planned murder rather than chivalric combat between two men of honor.

California duels were, as San Francisco historian Charles Dobie wrote, "often one of the sideshows in the great circus ring of politics, contests between two moral expediencies." This was certainly true of the Terry-Broderick gunfight. United States Senator David Broderick was a liberal Free Labor Democrat staunchly opposed to slavery while Federal Judge David Terry, though also a Democrat, was a hard line conservative who strongly advocated bringing slavery to California. Terry was a transplanted southern aristocrat, and Broderick was a man of the common people.

At this time in California's history, the state's Democratic party was split into two opposing factions, slavery and suffrage being the divisive issues. To the dismay of conservatives, the liberals, under the leadership of Broderick, were steadily growing more powerful and influential.

Senator Broderick was an extremely popular politician, highly respected by his constituents and was expected to win re-election by a landslide. He was also a very outspoken man, never afraid to speak the truth as he saw it. When Broderick publically denounced Terry for showing favoritism in his court decisions, the judge immediately challenged him to a duel. It seemed almost as if Terry had been waiting for just such an opportunity.

On a morning grey with fog, the two men rendezvoused on the lonely shore of Lake Merced just beyond the San Francisco city limits and faced each other with pistols brought to the site by Terry's party. On the count of one, Broderick's pistol discharged as he was raising it. The bullet kicked up dirt a mere ten feet in front of him. Instantly, Terry shot back, sending his own bullet right into Broderick's chest.

The senator rocked back on his heels, stood perfectly motionless for a few seconds, then dropped to the ground like a marionette whose strings had been cut. His seconds and a doctor rushed to his side. Finding him still alive, they placed him on a carriage and took him at once to a nearby hilltop mansion owned by a friend.

For hours, Broderick lingered near death. At the end of each hour, mounted couriers galloped off to San Francisco carrying bulletins on his condition. The bulletins were then placed outside the city's newspaper office, where crowds awaited the news. When the last bulletin arrived announcing the death of Senator David C. Broderick, men wept openly in the streets.

On the day of Broderick's funeral, nearly every store in San Francisco closed, whole buildings were draped with black banners, and thousands of mourners followed the cortege to Lone Mountain Cemetery. Broderick had scarcely been laid to rest before suspicions of foul play began to surface.

An examination of the gun Broderick used revealed it had a hair trigger which caused it to fire prematurely. It was also learned that Terry had practiced with both pistols on the day before the duel. Furthermore, a bartender named John Sloan claimed to have overheard Judge Terry tell some of his cronies, "We shouldn't have killed him. We only made him a martyr."

David Terry was brought to trial but the evidence against him was not substantial enough to convict and he went free.

Author Amelia Ransome Neville, who was a close friend of Broderick's, had a completely different theory about the senator's death. She believed he deliberately chose to fire into the ground because he could not bring himself to take another man's life. "Duels and killings were not in his philosophy," she wrote. Neville suggested that Broderick may have hoped to only receive a flesh wound, and though his luck was not with him that fateful morning, he died without violating his principles.

Whether Broderick was a victim of his own noble character or was brought down by a diabolical conspiracy remains an unsolved mystery. However, his slaying essentially ended California's dueling era. Public outrage over Broderick's death was so great that duels not only lost their glamour, but they came to be reviled.

The times were changing and more and more men were realizing that the wisest way to defend one's honor and ego was in a court of law. Libel suits came to be seen as a much less dangerous means of responding to intolerable defamation of character. The days when men preferred death before dishonor disappeared forever into the romantic mists of California's melodramatic history.

Bibliography - Chapter 7

Beck Warren A. and Williams, David A. **California. A History of the Golden State**. Garden City, New York. Doubleday & Company, Inc. 1972.

Cleland, Robert Glass. **A History of California: The American Period.** New York. Macmillan Company. 1992.

Davis, William Heath. **Sixty Years in California.** San Francisco. A.J. Leary, Publisher. 1889.

Romano, Margaret. *Frontier Times* magazine. Austin, Texas. Western Publication, Inc. June, 1985.

Secrest, William B. *True West* magazine. Austin, Texas. Western Publications. May, 1991.

8

"This Whole Damn Town Is Haunted!"

The ghost town of Bodie stands gaunt in the noonday sun. Every day its weather-beaten old buildings sag closer to the earth. Tumbleweeds roll down the streets, cast away by the forlorn hills to the north.

The two-story, bell-towered school house still squats on a side street, never again to echo with children's laughter, while the blunt old church waits in vain to hear once more the singing of joyous hymns.

Nothing remains of the old bank nowadays, except its aged, brick vault, solid as ever.

The general stores' shelves are still stocked with aged patent bottles and a dressmaker's mannikin which stands bare as if expecting to be clothed again in a Nineteenth Century gown at any moment.

Bodie remains as it has always been. It lacks only one thing —citizens. Bodie is a ghost town, and an exceptional one at that. It not only holds memories and memorabilia of the past, but, if one can believe all the stories one hears, it also hosts the ghosts of its previous residents.

Rarely a day goes by that a tourist who has been peeking through the windows and walking over the creaking floors of the buildings does not report a ghost sighting to one of the park rangers. And, more than likely, the ranger will smile and reply, "A ghost? Hell, mister, this whole damn town is haunted."

Perhaps it's not surprising that Bodie is full of ghosts. The past lingers here, forming a perfect setting for ghostly appearances of former inhabitants. Though some of Bodie's ghosts behave inexplicably and even rudely, most seem content to go about their spectral rituals oblivious of the living persons passing by all around them.

As mining camps went, Bodie was not all that special in appearance. It boasted no opera house and no millionaires' mansions. Still, in its heyday, the population was around 10,000, and it contained 60 saloons and seven breweries. Whorehouses lined Virgin Alley and Maiden Lane while opium was available in Chinatown.

Bodie was as wild and wicked as any frontier town anywhere. Perhaps the weather had something to do with it. At 8,300 feet, Bodie's winters were long and bitter, prompting people to say, "In Bodie, there's eleven months of winter and one month of hell." Bodie's many gunfights led to the nickname "Shooters' Town."

If Bodie was a wicked place, it was also a prosperous one. Bodie's great, gothic-looking brick stamp mill produced 900 pounds of gold amalgam a day. Stock in the Bodie mine rose from 40 cents a share in 1877 to one dollar on June 1, 1878, then shot up to $18 by August. This incredible surge made a lot of Bodie speculators "giddy-headed rich" overnight.

Life for the miners and mill workers was better than average as well. These laborers were paid four dollars a day during a time when a dollar a day was average. Prices were, of course, equally high. Firewood, so vital during the long, hard winters, ran as much as $25 a cord; a quart of milk was 50 cents, and, at the end of a long day's work, two drinks of whiskey could be had for a quarter.

One of Bodie's most prominent citizens at the time was James Stuart Cain, the mine and mill operator, a banker, and major property owner. Cain moved to Bodie with his wife, Martha Delilah, in 1879. They soon built one of the town's finest homes.

The Cain's wealth allowed them to hire a maid who was said to have been a lovely young Chinese woman. James and the maid became lovers, and when Martha found out, she fired the maid and sent her away from the house. Disgraced and humiliated, the young woman committed suicide. Her ghost is often seen standing mournfully in the upper bedroom of the Cain House.

A much more frightening apparition has also been encountered here. During the 1970s, Ranger Ken Fetherston and his wife, Elizabeth, lived in the

Cain house for a couple of years. One night, they were sleeping in the lower bedroom when Elizabeth felt a heavy pressure upon her. It was almost as if someone powerful was on top of her.

Frightened almost out of her wits, she fought wildly and wound up landing on the floor. Upon recovering on the floor, the pressure ceased.

Others have experienced this disturbing phenomena. One evening, Midge Reddon, administrative officer of the State Park's Sierra District, and her husband, Bob, stayed in a different house down the street from the Cain's place. They had just turned in for the night. As Bob was about to fall asleep, he felt something begin to push down on him.

His legs and arms were pinned so that he could not move them; he could not raise his head, and he felt as if he was going to suffocate. Bob struggled desperately until, at last, he was able to let out a yell. His shout awakened his wife and drove the phantom away.

Were Bob Reddon's and Elizabeth Fetherston's terrifying experiences simply extreme nightmares or is there something malevolent that prowls from house to house at night in Bodie?

Most of Bodie's ghosts pay little or no attention to the living. They are much too busy with their own concerns. One of the busiest ghosts is that of Whitney Chidester.

Originally, Chidester was a Sacramento bank cashier who routinely handled large sums of money. Over a period of several years, he quietly and carefully embezzled thousands of dollars. When his stash reached $27,000, he left town and headed for Bodie to hole up unnoticed in the bustling mine camp.

Chidester moved into a humble shack and pretended to be a hermit. He let his beard grow long,

BODIE'S CHURCH. This gaunt old church waits for darkness to bring forth the ghost town's multitudes of spectral inhabitants.

Desert Magazine Archive

wore ragged clothes, and ate cheap food. No one, he thought, would suspect he was a wealthy man with a small fortune tucked away inside a baking powder can. When the search for him ended, he would be able to move to San Francisco and live like a gentleman.

His disguise worked well for a while until some of the town's rougher elements noticed that, although the hermit spent very little money, he always managed to pay for his groceries and firewood in cash. They concluded that he must be a miser with money cached in his hovel.

One of Chidester's few friends in Bodie was Joe Stockton, a local blacksmith. The hermit liked to hang out in the warmth of the smithy's shop, and Stockton had grown protective of this odd, vulnerable derelict. One night in a saloon, Stockton overheard two men discussing plans to rob the hermit. He went at once to Chidester's shack and informed him of the plot. Whitney Chidester knew it was time to leave town.

As soon as Stockton left, Chidester grabbed his baking powder can and headed off the path down to the stagecoach stop. He was just a little too late; the thieves ambushed him before he got to the main street. They pummeled him and stabbed him with knives.

The thugs tore the tin can from his dead fingers, opened it, and poured out the contents —baking powder. In his haste, Chidester grabbed the wrong canister. Now, almost every night, his ghost returns to the ruins of his cabin to find the right baking powder canister.

Equally distraught is the restless ghost of Lottie Johl. Lottie's story is a touching one, as poignant as any of Bodie's frontier tales.

Lottie Johl was a whore. It is whispered that she

was a lovely woman, hazel eyed with curly, red hair. She worked in one of the most popular brothels in Bodie, and it was here that she met Eli Johl. Johl was as different from Lottie as night is from day. He was a big, awkward man, a butcher by trade who spoke broken English with a heavy German accent. He was a lonely man with few friends, so he often spent his evenings in the bordellos, where, for a price, he could be with women who accepted him as he was.

It is uncertain just when Eli Johl became one of Lottie's customers, but it was probably in 1879. Eli grew very fond of the young harlot. Not only did she take him to her bed, but she would dance with him and sometimes just sit and talk. Eli fell in love with Lottie and soon he asked to marry her. Lottie, who must have been longing for a more respectable life, accepted and the couple moved into Johl's humble house.

Lottie Johl longed for refinement in her new life. She played the piano so Eli bought her a fine one. She took up painting and Eli proudly framed her amateur pictures and hug them around the house. The young couple had hoped to be accepted by the community but this was not to be. Though they sent out invitations, no one came to hear Lottie play her piano or to view her artwork.

The Johls lived reclusively but happily for several years. Then, Lottie contracted one of Bodie's most dreaded illness —pneumonia— and died suddenly. The grief-stricken Eli wanted his wife to be buried in the town's cemetery, but the local gentry was opposed. Whores, they reminded Eli, were always buried outside the wrought iron fence of the graveyard. Eli protested. His wife had been good and faithful; her past did not matter. Finally, a compromise was reached. Lottie could be buried within the cemetery, but only in its farthest corner next to the fence.

Here, Lottie Johl lies today, still ostracized and looked down upon. Her lonely spirit is said to walk at night among the tombstones of the righteous citizens who had snubbed her so badly in life.

The saddest little ghost in the whole town is that of the small child known as "The Angel of Bodie." This little girl's name seems to be forgotten, but she may have been an orphan, because she spent her days tagging along with a construction worker as he toiled at his job. This laborer, Danny Cloverdale, was well-suited to be a father image to a neglected child. Cloverdale was thoughtful and caring of this little waif who followed him everywhere he went.

Then, one terrible day, Cloverdale swung his heavy miner's pick over his shoulder without looking behind him, struck the little girl on the head, and killed her on the spot. Cloverdale was nearly crazed with grief when he realized what he had done. The little girl was laid to rest in a tiny grave in the Bodie cemetery. Apparently, she haunts the grave to this day.

Not long ago, a family of tourists was exploring Bodie when their youngest daughter became separated from the group. The father found her on the outskirts of the old cemetery, prancing around, laughing and clapping her hands. When her father called to her, she came running. "Did you see my friend?" the girl exclaimed excitedly. "She was so pretty and she was wearing an old-timey dress just like in the picture book. I wonder where she went?"

The father, of course, saw nothing.

This was neither the first nor the last appearance of the "Angel of Bodie." In 1933, two employees of the Civilian Conservation Corps were sitting on a bench outside of the Miner's Union Hall when they both heard a child's voice cry out, "Danny?" The men looked around, but there were no children anywhere nearby. Then, they distinctly heard the voice a second time. "Danny?"

Mysterious voices are one of the most common ghostly phenomena in Bodie. Once, Bill Lindemann, museums coordinator for the State Park and Recreation Department's Tahoe-Sierra District, was staying overnight in the Medocini House when he began hearing a potpourri of strange voices. It sounded, he claimed, like "a radio when two stations are crossed. Like a party or a number of people speaking at once." Lindemann searched the house room by room but could not determine where the sounds were coming from. He went outdoors, but, although he could still hear the blurry voices, he could tell that they were not coming from any of the darkened houses nearby.

Finally, he returned to the Medocini place and shouted at the walls. "I'm sorry to break up your party but I'm trying to sleep," he yelled, and the noises stopped.

Strange noises come and go frequently at the Medocini House. Children's laughter is often heard, as are adult voices. Piano music sometimes drifts out of the museum after it has closed for the night and the tinkling of a music box has been reported in the empty Cain House.

The town of Bodie is so wonderfully enchanted that the old-time residents pretty much took the ghosts for granted. Bob Bell, who lived most of his life in Bodie, repeatedly saw a little old lady seated in a rocking chair working on an afghan in the deserted Gregory House. At the Dechambeau House he saw a woman peering from an upstairs window so often that he used to wave at her.

Why are so many ghosts concentrated in one little abandoned town? And why such variety? While some of the phantoms seem quite contented, most are very dissatisfied, still unhappy about the outcomes of their earthly lives. Perhaps, their discontent holds them back from entering the spiritual dimension. One can only guess and marvel at the most haunted town in the entire United States.

How to Visit the Haunted Town of Bodie

If arriving from Carson City, Nevada, take Highway 395 fifty miles south to Bridgeport, California and on to the Highway 270 turnoff. Turn east for six miles to a road heading northeast. Ten miles later, you will be in Bodie. When coming up from Bishop, drive north 75 miles on Highway 395, past Mono Craters and Mono Lake to the Highway 270 turnoff. Then drive on into the haunted past.

Bibliography - Chapter 8

Ballenger, Noella and Tulley, Jalien. *True West* magazine. Austin, Texas. Western Publications. April, 1991.

Holmes, Pat. *Desert* magazine. Palm Desert, California. October, 1968.

Loose, Warren. *Desert* magazine. Palm Desert, California. November-December, 1975.

Murbarger, Nell. *Desert* magazine. Palm Desert, California. October, 1960.

Myers, Arthur. The Ghostly Gazetteer. Chicago. Contemporary Books, Inc. 1990.

Ninnis, Lillian. *Desert* magazine. Palm Desert, California. October, 1960.

Tialiaferro, Charles R. *Desert* magazine. Palm Desert, California. December, 1978.

9

The Fire Eaters
of the Cahuillas

The great ceremonial fire had burned down to a bed of glowing embers. The people gathered on all four sides of the fire now grew hushed and expectant. Those closest to the flames were seated on benches and chairs. Behind them, rows of people stood, arms folded, waiting.

The rich mesquite wood smoke rose toward the full moon. Suddenly, a thin, wrinkled old man stepped from the shadows into the flickering circle of light. Though he was frail, he let out a leonine roar. "Who-huh!" Immediately, two other male chanters responded. "Huh! Huh!" The ancient chant had begun. The roar and the grunts were repeated over and over, faster and faster, until they became simultaneous. Then, as quickly as it started, the chant ended.

A fourth man strode in. Though he was dressed in simple clothes —a plain old jacket and faded blue jeans— he was obviously not an ordinary man. On his shoulders he wore the feathers of predatory birds; a soft, feathered headband encircled his forehead and the pockets of his ill-fitting coat were stuffed with curiously shaped rocks. He was a Cahuilla *pul* —a shaman of awesome power.

The audience was silent as he walked slowly around the smoldering fire. Although the shaman was wide-eyed, he stumbled unsteadily like a man emerging from a dream-filled sleep. He knelt by the fire and blew a tremendous breath on the smoking blaze. Instantly the fire flared up.

Four times, he blew on the flames, first from the east, then from the west and the south, and finally from the north. Next, he began stomping his foot on the ground, creating a sound much like a jackrabbit thumping out a warning. From his belt, he drew forth two owl feathers and brushed them through the rising heat wave to drive away any evil spirits that might be present.

The *pul* squatted again, picked around in the hot coals with his bare fingers and selected a bright red one. He placed it on the palm of his hand and stood back up. He raised his hand to his face, dropped the glowing ember onto his tongue, and, without flinching, closed his mouth. After inhaling deeply, he blew out a shower of sparks.

A loud murmur came from the crowd. This was what they had come to see —a human being actually eating fire. For most of the spectators, it was a deeply religious experience, a confirmation of their ancient beliefs. For the scattering of non-Indians on the edges of the crowd, it was a source of wonderment and considerable skepticism. Was this a genuine miracle or some form of trickery?

Whether miracle or trick, the second part of the ceremony was even more mystifying. The *pul* spat out the cold, black coal, knelt again, and coughed up something into the palm of his hand. He showed the object in the light of the fire, where it squirmed like a small, white grubworm. Everyone around him gasped, for they realized the shaman was holding his living soul in his hand. Quickly, the *pul* swallowed the squirming object and the ceremony abruptly ended.

The Cahuillas are one of the smaller, lesser-known North American Indian tribes but the magical powers of their shamans greatly exceeds those of the larger tribes. Indeed, they have needed the supernatural intervention of good spirits to survive in their harsh desert homeland situated on the northwest end of the Salton Sea.

A thousand years ago, life was remarkably good for the original Cahuillas. At that time, the Colorado River diverted its outlet from the Gulf of California to the Salton Sink creating an enormous prehistoric lake referred today as Lake Cahuilla. The lake shore became an oasis in an otherwise arid land, a very suitable place for primitive people to live.

There was the luxury of an unlimited quantity of fresh water and abundant vegetation —willows, palm trees, and mesquite— grew along the shoreline. This wooded area attracted birds, small game animals, and, best of all, plenty of fish. With fish traps, the Cahuillas became expert fishermen of the desert. They lived well for many generations.

Then the fickle Colorado River changed her mind. She decided to transfer her waters back to the Gulf of California again and abandon Lake Cahuilla. The once-great body of water dried up. Now, the Cahuillas were faced with a much more hostile landscape. They were, nonetheless, a resourceful people who adapted quite well to their new surroundings.

Their most impressive accomplishment was the digging and maintaining of wells, large pits which were accessed by sloping trenches. Their homes were simple but ingenious structures, brush-covered A-frames called *kishes*.

The Cahuillas diet consisted largely of mesquite beans supplemented by an occasional meal of venison or rabbit stew. Moccasins were made of deer skins and graceful pottery was made from clay. It was a hard and simple life, but, with spiritual guidance from the holy *puls*, the Cahuillas survived season after season.

Today, they live on the vast, 24,000-acre Torres Martinez Indian Reservation, straddling the line between the modern world and the ancient one.

Traditionally, a *pul's* power came through dreaming. A potential *pul*, sensing his "differentness," would go off into the desert wilderness to a quiet spot. There he would take powerful hallucinogenic drugs made from the jimson weed and the elephant tree, and soon enter a dream-like state.

Once on the first level of dreaming, the young *pul* would force his or her self to fall asleep within the dream and awaken in the next higher level. In this way, as many as 14 levels of dreaming could be reached to give a *pul* full visionary and healing powers.

These transitions were not without risk. A would-be *pul* could easily get lost in a dream, be unable to return, and go into a coma. When this happened, an older and wiser *pul* would have to enter the young one's dreams and guide the lost soul back out.

On one of the dream levels, the aspiring *pul* would meet a spirit guide, usually in the form of a bird

LEGENDARY SHAMAN. The Cahuilla shaman known as "Basket" as he looked in 1949. His fiery magic produced miraculous cures when modern medical science failed.

Field Studio/Riverside, California

or animal such as an owl, eagle, or mountain lion. This creature would give the *pul* both guidance and power throughout the rest of the shaman's life.

The *puls* soon learned that everything on earth has a spirit, not only humans and animals but plants and even rocks. This knowledge put them in direct touch with all the spirit forces of the cosmos.

The healing and visionary powers of the *puls* helped the Cahuillas through many difficult times and gave them a better understanding of the changing world around them. For example, when World War II broke out, the Cahuillas could not understand why their young men were being ordered to register for the draft. They had never heard of the place called Pearl Harbor and knew nothing about the distant nation of Japan. Why should their sons be called to fight against these foreign people who lived so far away?

They took this question to a *pul* named Basket and he promised to ask the spirits for an answer. Basket participated in a fire-lit chant, at the end of which he dropped to his knees and pounded the hard-packed earth with his fist. The sound was so powerful that people standing nearly a mile away claimed to have heard it.

Next, Basket pressed his ear to the ground. For several long minutes, he listened without moving. He rose to his feet and announced that he had been in touch with the Earth God, the god of their fathers and of all growing things. The god had told them that their country was indeed endangered, that evil was sweeping across the seas and that it was their duty to go out and protect their lands and their homes and do whatever was asked of them by their white brothers.

With this revelation, the young Cahuilla men dutifully registered for the draft while some promptly joined the Marines. During the next three years, they fought gallantly in the Pacific war but those that survived the hell of Tarawa and Iwo Jima came home psychologically damaged men. They were tortured by depression and nightmares. Government doctors diagnosed them as suffering from battle fatigue; they recommended rest and quiet. Time would heal them, they were told. Still, the men got no better.

The local *pul* took charge. In a ceremonial hut tucked away in the brush, the medicine man named Basket —the same shaman who had sent these men off to war— decided to bring them home from it by performing a fire-eating ritual.

The ceremony began in the usual way. With two of the former soldiers seated by the fire, a chant was performed. Following this, Basket approached the men and brushed them with wands of owl feathers, especially around the head, neck and shoulders. Occasionally, he shook the feathers over the fire as if he was flicking something away by the gesture.

Next, he placed two red-hot coals in his mouth and blew sparks on each veteran until the embers turned cold and black. Then, Basket knelt, placing his lips over one of the patient's lips and blew very hard. The young man's cheeks puffed out and his eyes bulged from the force of the blast but he did not flinch.

The *pul* went on to blow in his nostrils and finally very hard in each ear. Lastly, grasping him by the ears, he drew the man's forehead to him and put his lips on a spot just above and directly in between the eyes. He sucked hard before pulling his mouth away with a resounding pop and he spat something into his hand —a small, white squirming object which he then cast into the fire.

Basket performed the same process with a

second youth, with the same results. Then, the great *pul* made a short speech. He said that while engaged in combat, these boys had been invaded by the newly-released spirits of some enemy soldiers they had killed. Those spirits penetrated their souls and were determined to torment them for the rest of their lives. Instead, they had been destroyed by the Cahuilla fire.

Naturally, most if not all non-Indian doctors were utterly disbelieving of such miraculous cures. They attributed the healings to the power of suggestion, that the young men's faith was so strong that psychological cures took place. On the other hand, fire eating is more difficult to explain.

It is true that fire eating is an ancient art. Indeed, it has long been presented on stages as a magic trick and religious mystics have often performed remarkable feats of fire handling to impress their followers. Fire immunity can be achieved in a number of ways, and the Cahuilla methods seem to be largely a case of mind over matter.

According to the *puls*, the secret to ritual fire eating is to "think yourself hot first." Casimiro, a legendary *pul* of the 1940s and 1950s, once told historian John Hilton: "It is easy to eat fire if you believe you can. During the chant, you must think your hand very warm, then very hot, then hotter than fire. When your hand is hotter than fire, fire feels cool. You can handle it very easily.

"Next, think your tongue and mouth very hot the same way." With a laugh, Casimiro added, "Then, fire tastes just like ice cream."

Though he was very unsure of himself, Hilton decided to give it a try. Using all his concentration, he thought his hand hot and was able to handle the coals, but when he placed an ember in his mouth, he instantly blistered his tongue.

Again, Casimiro laughed. "There was no chant," he said. "You can't eat fire without the chanting."

Not all *puls* have used their power for good and religious purposes; some have sought to make money from their extraordinary talents. One young Indian once dressed in Hollywood feathers and performed fire dances for the public at $50 per show. His fellow Cahuillas despised him for it. At the next real fire-eating ceremony, everything was done deliberately wrong. The timing was off; the chants were improperly sung and nothing worked right.

When the climactic moment came, the false *pul* fumbled a coal into his mouth and was severely burned. This was considered just punishment by the other Cahuillas.

Unfortunately, the 10,000 year era of great Cahuilla shamanism —whether exploited or pure— has passed. The last great *pul*, Ruby Modesto, died in 1989 and there is no one left to take her place.

With Modesto's death, 10 centuries of oral tradition were lost forever; she knew songs, chants,and stories that were known by no one else. Her widower, David Modesto, has struggled to preserve as many fragments of his culture as possible. For a time, he taught Cahuilla language classes in a federally-funded program but a mere 10 students enrolled. "I guess kids nowadays like pop music more than old songs," Modesto lamented.

Still, David Modesto refuses to give up the hope that a new *pul* will arise some day and revive the ancient powers. "*Puls* are born, not taught," he said. "It is only necessary for a man or woman to dream the dreams of a *pul* in order to make the connection to the spirit world which pervades all things."

So, perhaps somewhere in the land of the Cahuillas, a child is dreaming tonight. Maybe, Ruby Modesto will appear in that dream to become the spirit guide of that child, to lead him or her to that state of perfection which allows *puls* to listen and speak to gods, perform miraculous healings, see visions, and to eat fire.

Bibliography - Chapter 9

Aleshare, Peter. *Desert* magazine. Palm Desert, California. December, 1981.

Hilton, John. *Desert* magazine. Palm Desert, California. May, 1949.

Hoyt, Franklin. *Desert* magazine. Palm Desert, California. July, 1956.

Lawbaugh, A. La Vielle. *Desert* magazine. Palm Desert, California. September, 1949.

McDonald, Russ. *True West* magazine. Austin, Texas. Western Publications. November, 1991.

McKenney, J. Wilson. *Desert* magazine. Palm Desert, California. November, 1950.

Shumway, Nina Paul. *Desert* magazine. Palm Desert, California. January, 1961.

Weight, Harold O. *Desert* magazine. Palm Desert, California. March, 1952.

10

The Search for Pegleg's Black Gold

In the burnt-out, wrinkled-up wasteland beyond the Salton Sea lie the eternally wild Borrego Badlands and the Santa Rosa Mountains. Within these wild lands rests a treasure of immeasurable value, a treasure that has taunted generations of adventurous men to the edge of madness for more than a century and a half.

Of all the Golden Gate State's countless spellbinding lost treasure tales, none has captured the searchers' imaginations more than the story of the Lost Pegleg Gold Mine. The most tantalizing aspect of this legend is that no digging is required to recover the gold. Not even a pick and shovel are needed.

The original discovery of Pegleg's Golden Hill was made by John O. Smith in either 1829 or 1836. Smith was traveling with some companions from Yuma to Los Angeles. For unknown reasons, they were not following the regular route.

Three days up from the Colorado River, the party camped at the base of three small hills in the middle of nowhere. Smith climbed the lowest hill to get a look at the lay of the land ahead. Around his feet, he found an abundance of odd-looking black pebbles unlike any he had seen before. Mildly curious, he gathered a handful to take down and show to his friends.

These men were horse traders, not miners. They had no knowledge of precious minerals, and informed Smith that he had probably found copper. Smith apparently thought this was worth remembering, because he kept samples. More than a decade would go by before he would learn their true value.

In 1848, gold was discovered in California and the whole state went crazy. The gold mania made John Smith wonder what he had actually found so many years ago in those distant hills. He had his pebbles assayed and learned that, when the black desert varnish was removed, there was gold underneath. Smith then realized that he had stumbled upon a bonanza, but had unknowingly walked away from it. Now, he vowed to go back.

John O. Smith was one of the more colorful characters of his time. With his curly beard and fringed leather jacket, he looked more like a mountain man than a desert rat. He was a rambling man, not content to stay in one place for too long. After he sold a herd of horses in Los Angeles, he wandered off into southern Utah.

Here, he moved in with an Indian tribe. Smith had no use for his straight-laced Mormon neighbors but he did like their custom of polygamy. He married five Indian women and cared for them well in his roughshod way.

John Smith had two weaknesses: stealing horses and drinking whiskey. As a rustler, he was a successful man; as a drunk he was someone to stay away from. Whenever he was under the influence of liquor, which was often, he was wild, mean, and dangerous.

Around 1848, Smith said goodbye to his Indian wives and joined a wagon train headed for California. Near Mountain Meadows, Utah, the migrants ran into a band of hostile Indians. In the fight that ensued, Smith was hit in the lower leg by an arrow. The wound became infected, and the leg had to be amputated below the knee.

Legend has it that Smith himself, fortified with whiskey, cut off his leg using a belt knife and carpenter's saw. In reality, the operation was performed by the wagon train's doctor, surgeon Jonathan Tibbet. The doctor also carved a wooden leg for his patient. Hence, John Smith became known as Pegleg Smith.

By 1854, Pegleg had organized a large expedition to go back to his golden hill. The venture ended in failure, however. Pegleg Smith could not remember his exact route; it had just been too many years. Pegleg mounted a second expedition in 1856 but, it, too was unsuccessful.

By now, a good many people were having serious doubts about this loud-mouthed, drunken horse thief who promised so much but could deliver nothing. And many others also questioned the very existence of a hill where gold lay on the ground waiting to be picked up by hand.

Gold is a heavy metal. It gravitates downward, sometimes all the way down to bedrock. The chances of nuggets lying out in the open are slim.

Still, there is a way it could happen. The land where Pegleg made his strike was once under Lake Cahuilla. Since the dessication of this inland sea, there has been considerable seismic uplift and tilting of the whole region. Tremblor-tantrums are felt occasionally on the three distinct fault lines that crack the landscape. This could explain the nuggets being on high ground.

Next, wind becomes a factor. Gale force winds known as *chubascos* sometimes roar across the desert, literally sandblasting the land to uncover the golden nuggets. Then, the strange biochemical process of patination or desert varnish takes place and the nuggets are neatly camouflaged in black. It all seems unlikely but is far from impossible.

The possibility that Pegleg's "mine" did really exist continued to send men out in search of it, but these expeditions always ended in tragedy rather than triumph. In 1863, a man who called himself "McGuire" showed up in San Francisco boasting that he had found the lost Pegleg mine. As proof, he displayed several blackened nuggets roughly the size of walnuts. Within a few weeks, McGuire led a group of five adventurers off to seek the gold. Several months passed before their bleaching bones were found half buried in the desert sands by a wandering prospector. McGuire's party had not only failed to find the gold, but were also unable to locate the waterholes along the way.

In the 1880s, a party headed by a man named Breedlove met a similar fate. The expedition was out-fitted for a month's journey, and, when they failed to return at the appointed time, a rescue team was sent out. The searchers found the party in the broiling wasteland not far from the Mexican border. All had died of dehydration.

No organized expedition ever found the lost gold field but two accidental discoveries did occur, both times by local Indians.

In 1876, while the Southern Pacific Railroad was building its line across the Salton Basin, an Indian woman staggered onto the construction site, nearly dead. When she recovered, she told a strange, sad story.

She and her husband had been traveling on foot from the Rio San Luís Rey Indian Reservation to another reservation near Yuma. One day, they climbed one of three low hills for a look around. To their sur-prise and delight, they saw that the hilltop was lit-tered with blackened gold nuggets.

The couple eagerly filled a bandanna with the precious metal and headed on. In the morning, they discovered that their canteen had begun to leak. The husband insisted that his wife drink what little water they had left. He died within days.

The woman plodded on until she sighted the train's plume of smoke and continued on to safety. She untied her bandanna, showed the workers her wealth and went on her way, never to be seen again.

A few years later, a half-breed known as Red Jim displayed a similar stash of black gold to his employers at the Warner Ranch west of the Borrego

Badlands. Jim was a cowboy who spent his free time exploring the badlands and the San Ysidro Mountains. During one of his many forays, he found the fabled hill.

On each of his trips, Jim apparently took only enough gold to tide him over for awhile. Perhaps he feared he would be robbed. In any event, he was a secretive man who let no one other than his wife know the location of his bonanza.

On at least one occasion, Jim did take his wife, Carmelita, along with him to help comb the hillside for nuggets. Probably, he felt she was the one person he could trust to know the route.

Red Jim did not spend his money extravagantly, although he spent some of it on whiskey, for he got into a drunken brawl one evening and was stabbed to death. The following day, Carmelita found $4,000 hidden away in his bunk.

The other ranch hands questioned her about the treasure. Would she be willing, they asked, to guide them to the site for half the profits? She quickly agreed.

"If we leave at dawn, we can camp at the Spring of the White Ledge," Carmelita said. "Next day, we go till the sun is straight overhead. We will then be at the place of the golden rocks."

Just a day and a half's ride to a fabulous treasure. It sounded too good to be true —and it was. Carmelita not only could not find her husband's gold-laden hillside, but she could not find the White Ledge waterhole either. After two nights of dry camps, the cowboys called it quits and retreated back to the Warner Ranch.

These tales at least narrowed the search. The treasure obviously lay between the Southern Pacific

Railroad line and the Warner Ranch, which was a landmark on the old Butterfield Stagecoach Road. The problem was that this still covered an area of 50 miles in width; the only real value to this new information was that it told people where not to look.

Time went by and the quest went on, but the gold remained as elusive as a desert mirage. Then one day in the spring of 1965, 130 years after Pegleg made his original discovery, an anonymous letter arrived at the offices of *Desert* magazine in Palm Desert, California. When the editor, Choral Pepper, opened the envelope, a blackened gold nugget the size of a quarter slid out onto her desk. Inside the envelope was a handwritten letter signed simply: "Sincerely yours, The Man Who Found Pegleg's Black Gold."

Desert magazine was a fine and folksy periodical which, between 1940 and 1984, published well-researched articles about desert flora, fauna, geology, and history. In 1965, *Desert* had featured a detailed story about Pegleg and his fantastic gold strike.

The article had prompted this anonymous writer to respond. "It is time once and for all to end the mystery, the speculation, and the controversy," the author wrote. "Almost ten years ago, I found what is known as the 'burned gold of Pegleg.' Without pinpointing the discovery on a map for reasons that are obvious, I will say only that it is less than 30 miles from the Salton Sea.

"I've gone back to the location an average of twice a year since the first discovery, and, according to my records, I've brought back and sold a total of $314,650 worth of Pegleg's black gold nuggets. The money had been wisely and quietly invested.

"Why then, should I break a ten-year silence and write about this discovery now? For all these years, I've intended to keep the discovery an absolute secret for the rest of my life but now that I'm retired with a comfortable income to do with as I please, the passion for secrecy is no longer so important.

"Secondly, I've already found all the gold that can be easily collected without actual mining operations. With the surface gold gone, I don't think anyone else is going to find the Pegleg gold for the simple reason that whatever gold left is well underground.

"Finally, perhaps it is also time to give hope to those hardy souls who have spent months and years of their lives searching for lost bonanzas. There have always been doubting Thomases who claim the lost treasures of the desert are but figments of somebody's imagination. Well, I have proof that at least one lost desert bonanza has been found —and not lost again, for I know exactly where it is!"

The anonymous man then proceeded to tell how he made his fabulous discovery.

First, he clarified that he was a simple rockhound, not a hunter of treasures and lost mines. He loved the desert for itself; his biggest thrills were the finding of geodes or fields of springtime desert wildflowers. Other treasures were far from his mind.

One brisk day in March of 1955, the letter writer drove more or less randomly into the badlands. After parking his Jeep at the base of a low rocky hill, he strolled leisurely up the slope looking for interesting rock specimens. After a couple of miles of tramping, he sat down on the coarse, gravelly hillside to rest for a minute. As he gazed at the pastel landscape spreading out below him, he casually flicked pebbles down the slope with his thumb and forefinger the way a schoolboy shoots marbles.

Suddenly, he stopped. He had picked up a little

stone that was heavier than the rest of the bits of gravel. It was about twice the size of his thumbnail and was oxidized completely black.

Curious, he scraped the stone with his pocket knife and a dull yellow glinted through. The rockhound was scarcely breathing now, realizing he was holding a gold nugget in his hand. He scrambled around, brushing at the gravel, until he found another, then another.

Within the next two hours, the excited man had scratched out seven more nuggets which later weighed out from half an ounce on up to nearly two ounces. The dazed fellow sat down to gather his wits. He had obviously stumbled onto a fortune. What was he to do now?

The last thing he wanted was to lose what he had found by driving away half-cocked and not be able to find his way back, as had happened to the others before him. So, as he made his way down the hillside, he built rock cairns at 50 foot intervals to mark his passage. Then, he retraced his route to be sure it was adequate to follow.

It was nearly dark when he reached his Jeep for the second time. Having hiked a good eight miles altogether, the man was tired enough to be contented to spread his sleeping bag on the ground, though his excitement kept him awake most of the night.

In the morning, he built another cairn at the spot where his Jeep was parked, and, keeping a close eye on his odometer, drove back to the nearest rut road. After marking this turnoff with still another inconspicuous cairn, he proceeded on to the highway. Here, with the memory of his find still fresh in his mind, he sat in his vehicle and drew a map. He was feeling very secure when he headed for home.

The drive gave the wily prospector plenty of time to think. He decided to keep his "mine" a complete secret; he would not even file a claim. He was also reluctant to pay taxes on his gains, for, as he said in his letter, "the government spends too many taxpayers dollars on welfare for lazy beatniks."

Desert magazine published the anonymous man's letter in its March 1965 issue. Immediately, many treasure hunters responded with letters of their own. Most were congratulatory, some were skeptical, and a few begged for additional clues.

"The Man Who Found Pegleg's Gold" continued to write to *Desert*, and, in each letter, he included a small black piece of gold to prove his authenticity. He claimed to still have more than $25,000 worth of unsold nuggets stashed away.

In his second letter, the gold finder told of his subsequent trips to his lonely desert hill. After the first trip, he always went equipped with a metal detector which enabled him to locate bits of gold several inches below the surface. These nuggets were larger than those found on the ground; one huge one weighed 14.8 ounces. With a minimum of effort, he was reaping a modest fortune from a bleak, nondescript desert hillside lost amid scores of identical hills.

Then, in 1968, a surprise package arrived at the *Desert* offices. Inside, along with the usual nugget, was a curious and interesting artifact. The accompanying letter explained what the object was and how it came to be in the writer's possession.

The author had gone back to his diggings for one last visit. Though he was sure he had gleaned all the available gold, he wanted to check the surrounding area to be certain he had missed nothing. As he walked, carefully scrutinizing the ground, he spied something protruding an inch or two from the soil. A sweep of the metal detector revealed it to be metallic.

The man knelt, pulled the object from the sand, and brushed it off. To his astonishment, it proved to be the hilt section of a very old Spanish sword scabbard. The scabbard itself was made of iron but the decorative band around the center with rings attached appeared to be silver. It had not corroded like the iron portion had.

The back of the silver band was plain and smooth but the front was decorated with the image of a Spanish soldier holding a small child as if to say goodbye to his family before going off to war. Did this artifact mean the original discoverers and losers of the gold were Spanish explorers?

The anonymous letter writer speculated that they may have been members of the Peralta family. Luís María Peralta was one of Alta California's earliest settlers, the owner of two enormous land grants, one in California, the other in what is now Arizona. The Peraltas made their fortune primarily my mining silver but they also explored for gold.

Does this mean that Pegleg's gold field should properly be called Peralta's Lost Gold? Perhaps, but no one will ever know.

The black gold field still remains shrouded in mystery. To this day, its location is unknown. The Man Who Found Pegleg's Gold has continued to conceal his (or her) identity. It is likely he is deceased now. If so, he may have taken his secret to the grave with him.

It is also possible that the site is protected in still another way. Recently, a substantial part of California's deserts was designated by Congress as

Wilderness Areas. Under the Federal Wilderness Act of 1964, no mining is allowed. If, for example, the Golden Hill is within the Borrego Badlands, any underground gold deposits are safe now and forever.

And so the desert wins again. She gave mankind nearly 200 years to search for her greatest treasures but man took only what lay in the open, ignoring whatever gold may be underground. And now, it is too late. The real Pegleg bonanza may be forever unclaimed.

Bibliography - Chapter 10

Anonymous. *Desert* magazine. Palm Desert, California. March, 1965. May, 1965. December, 1965. August-September, 1966. December, 1967. July, 1968.

Buck, Robert. *Desert* magazine. Palm Desert, California. June, 1966.

Jasper, James. *Desert* magazine. Palm Desert, California. March, 1957.

Lentz, J.A. *Desert* magazine. Palm Desert, California. May,1968.

Marquiss, Kenneth. *Desert* magazine. Palm Desert, California. September, 1964.

Pepper, Choral. *Desert* magazine. Palm Desert, California. April, 1968.

Southworth, John. *Desert* magazine. Palm Desert, California. April, 1965.

Splinter, Henry. *Desert* magazine. Palm Desert, California. May, 1954.

11

Close Encounters–
California Style

"Oaklanders Saw Mystic Flying Light," blared a newspaper headline. "Hundreds believe an airship hovered over them. Say they saw a dark body above the gleam. It was headed for San Francisco and seemed about to come to Earth."

The front page of a contemporary supermarket tabloid? No, these headlines appeared in the respectable *San Francisco Call* on November 23,

143

1896, a century ago during an era when hot air balloons were the only known means of flight.

California has always been in the forefront of UFO sightings and contacts. In a state so avant-garde, this is not surprising. Back when the rest of the world was only beginning to dream of controlled, manned flight above and beyond earth, Californians were already witnessing it, and in a most spectacular way.

The great flying lights flap of 1896 began, interestingly enough, several hundred miles away from California. On the crisp, clear night of August 12, a luminous ball of fire glowing within a halo of multicolored lights approached the small town of Rossland, British Columbia at a high altitude.

The bright aerial body paused momentarily above a nearby mountain top, made several circles in the sky, then sped away.

Since the Rossland area was lightly populated, the incident was not widely publicized. Not many people in California even heard about this extraordinary event. Then, when the same odd light showed up above their towns and cities, hundreds of Californians sat up and paid close attention.

The first California sightings of the "wandering apparition," as the newspaper dubbed it, came on the night of November 17, 1896 over Sacramento. The sky was heavily overcast, so most observers reported seeing only a bright light moving slowly through the night. Others, however, swore they could see a dark body above the illumination. Five days later, when the mystery light sailed majestically over Oakland, the sky was clear and hundreds of gawking citizens were sure they saw something over the light. However, descriptions of this "supporting structure" varied, described as "cigar shaped," "egg shaped," or "barrel shaped."

Some possible explanations were advanced. Since a particularly spectacular object had flashed across the Bay Area skies a few weeks earlier, many folks assumed that this high-flying object was simply a second meteor. Others felt that the light was a lantern suspended from a hot air balloon which drifted on air currents above the cities.

No one who had actually seen the "phantom airship" accepted either theory. If the light was merely a floating lantern, who had launched it? And why? Was it just an elaborate prank of some sort? Subsequent sightings made both explanations seem highly unlikely.

Before November ended, 21 cities and towns, including San Jose, San Francisco, and Los Angeles, were visited by the nomadic luminosity. It shone like a ball of red, white, and blue fire as it drifted leisurely on its way. The most interesting observation of all was made by two Methodist ministers who claimed to have seen a fiery object sitting on the ground emitting brilliant rays of light. When the pastors attempted to approach the thing, it rose and took off in a slow, slanted flight path.

A fascinating report also came in from Tacoma, Washington, where a resident reported a strange object hovering over Mount Rainier shooting out beams of colored light in every direction, like spokes on a wheel. For over an hour, the weird craft "moved about with a waving motion, swayed back and forth and darted from one position to another."

In early December, a prominent San Francisco lawyer, George D. Collins, announced he knew the answer to the riddle of the widely-traveling mystery light. He told the press about a client who had approached him seeking advice about patenting procedures. The client, whom Collins declined to name, was an inventor. He displayed an impressive set of blueprints and boasted of strong financial backing. His invention, he said proudly, was the "world's first practical airship."

His aeroplane was almost operational and he would soon be secretly making test flights. After he received advice on how to make a patent application, he left Collins' office and did not return.

After the *San Francisco Call* printed Collins' story, public interest in airships skyrocketed. Everyone eagerly waited for the dazzling contraption to land and be revealed to the general public. Of course, this never happened, and one can only guess at the reasons why. Something spectacular flew all over the California countryside in late November of 1896. If it was man made, why was it never presented publicly? An invention of this magnitude, if it was not a lighter than air craft, would have sent the Wright brothers back to their bicycle shop. Why was it never unveiled?

The most likely answer is that it never existed, that the exuberant inventor was a flim-flam man selling investments in an invention that never got off the ground.

So, if the light was not of earthly origin, just where did it come from? Californians nervously turned their eyes to the stars.

Many works of popular fiction were based on the premise that Mars was an inhabited planet. The Martians were depicted as fierce, war-loving creatures with spaceships capable of attacking Earth. A lot of people became convinced that the flying light was a scout ship and the "War of the Worlds" was about to begin. Apparently there were no panics but there was considerable relief when the light quit making its nocturnal journeys.

This, of course, would not be California's last encounter with a UFO. During the exciting times that followed World War II when thousands of flying saucers and cigar-shaped mother ships were being seen worldwide, California reported an extraordinary number of extremely unusual sightings. And, more importantly, the state led the nation in people who allegedly made actual contact with the occupants of the UFOs.

The first such contactee was George W. Van Tassel. A veteran pilot, Van Tassel was the manager of Giant Rock Airport, a small general aviation facility in a remote part of the California desert. His first contact with extraterrestrials came one day in 1952 when he went into a trance-like state while sitting at the base of the huge, 50-foot boulder for which the base is named.

A huge flying saucer arrived and Van Tassel was teleported on board, where he was greeted by several aliens who gave him a guided tour of the ship's interior and explained the reason why the space ships continuously circle the Earth. The aliens were profoundly disturbed by the course of human history, and they wanted to bring enlightened change and peaceful ways to their wayward interplanetary neighbors.

The space travelers informed Van Tassel that some humans were partly non-terrestrial in origin and that these specially-bred people, along with many other carefully selected individuals, were being covertly contacted to be taught "the unseen truths of life" so they could pass these truths on to the people of Earth.

The aliens believed the contactees needed to

compete for the minds of mankind with new ideas instead of thinking only of new methods of mass destruction. Van Tassel returned to Giant Rock a very inspired man.

Van Tassel's second contact took place on August 24, 1952 while he and his wife were camped out in the desert. It was well after midnight when he was awakened by an unearthly being who called himself "Solgonda". Van Tassel crawled out of his sleeping bag, and, while his wife still slept, he accompanied Solgonda inside the flying saucer hovering nearby.

Once on board, Van Tassel outlined a plan he had for bringing together as many contactees as possible in one place at one time. He proposed holding a national flying saucer convention at Giant Rock Airport in the spring. For one full week, there would be meetings, seminars and planning sessions. For the first time ever, UFOlogists from all parts of the nation could gather to compare their experiences.

The first annual Giant Rock Space Convention was a grand success. Hundreds of UFO buffs showed up, and the event took on an old-time meeting atmosphere. Tables and booths were set up to bring in money selling pamphlets, buttons, and bumper stickers. For 17 years, the Giant Rock Space Convention was America's most unusual outdoor event. Between conventions, the Sage of Giant Rock kept very busy. Over a period of 20 years, Van Tassel appeared on more than 400 radio and television shows and gave nearly 300 lectures in the United States and Canada, as well as writing four popular books. He claimed that flying saucers often flashed their lights at him or flew in formation as they passed over Giant Rock in a salute just to him.

One man who never failed to attend the conventions was a colorful, middle-aged fellow named Orfeo Angelucci. This exuberant but unpretentious man claimed his first contact with a flying saucer occurred at age 46 in 1952. Angelucci was working the night shift at Lockheed's aircraft plant in Burbank, when, on the evening of May 23, he began to feel ill.

Angelucci left work early, around 11 p.m. He was driving unsteadily along the bank of the Los Angeles River when he noticed he was being followed by a glowing disc. The low flying saucer came closer and closer, and finally pulled alongside Angelucci's car, forcing him off the road.

Angelucci climbed out of his automobile in a daze to meet a "supra-humanly splendid man and woman" who had come by saucer from another world. The couple offered Angelucci a crystal goblet and, when he drank it, his illness was instantly gone.

He was then informed that, though he was a humble worker, he had been chosen to be one of the intermediaries between extraterrestrials and the people of Earth. He had been identified as one of those few mortals innately capable of receiving and transmitting wisdom from the stars.

The aliens spoke of their compassion for humanity and their sorrow over the needless suffering of mankind. Angelucci, they said, was to become one of their spokespersons, an evangelist who would spread their message across the nation.

Over the years that followed the first contact, Orfeo Angelucci met with his space friends many times. He claimed to have been taken on board the flying saucers and to have ridden in outer space. Though he was a happily married man with a family, he eventually entered into a "mystical marriage" with a spacewoman named Lyra.

Throughout the 1950s, Angelucci lectured constantly and wrote a book titled *Secrets of the Saucers*. Though he could offer no proof that his experiences were real, his humble sincerity made many listeners believe he was indeed telling the truth.

In 1960, the Giant Rock convention had the honor of hosting a presidential candidate as one of its speakers. The hopeful young politician was Gabriel Green, an independent candidate running for President of the United States on the Universal Party ticket.

Green was the founder-president of the Amalgamated Flying Saucer Club of America Inc. (AFSCA). He claimed to have seen many UFOs and to have been taken on board more than once by highly advanced beings from Venus, Mars, and Saturn. These space people had asked him to run for political office "in an effort to plant the seeds of needed reforms on our world."

Green decided to start at the top; he launched a campaign for president of the United States.

At the Giant Rock convention, he held a rally so people could hear "Gabriel blow his horn." Tickets were one dollar, so anyone who wanted "the World of Tomorrow today and Utopia now" could listen to a man who promised "The True Stairway to the Stars."

"America needs a Space Age President," Green told the gathering. He explained that he was the vocal telepathic channel for the "Space Masters and the Spiritual Hierarchy of Earth." He advocated a universal non-monetary economic system and a united theocratic world government patterned after those of other advanced planets. Green pledged an administration which would tell the people the truth about UFOs rather than keep them "in ignorance of the most vital information in all history."

For some reason, Gabriel Green's campaign never really took off. So, before the primaries he withdrew from the campaign and threw his support to John F. Kennedy. Green's political career, however, was far from over; in 1962, he ran for United States Senate.

His campaign focused on opposition to nuclear testing and stressed "new ideas instead of bombs and bullets." Surprisingly, he got 171,000 votes in the Democratic primary. Though it was not enough to win the nomination, it gave him hope. Green ran for President once again in 1972 but his campaign fizzled embarrassingly. The country was just not quite ready for a President who embellished his campaign literature with pictures of flying saucers and rocket ships instead of donkeys or elephants.

Remarkable stories continued to be told at the annual conventions. One of the many topics in 1954 was the subject of "angel's hair." This gossamer substance drifts out of the skies in great quantities, showering the land and sea with long, thin strands of cobweb-like material. It often appears in conjunction with UFO sightings.

Cobweb storms are rare phenomena but very impressive when they do happen. They have occurred worldwide, but an exceptional number of these events have taken place in California. The experience of W.J. Daily in Puente was a typical example.

On a bright, sunny February morning in 1954, Mrs. Daily was watching some jet planes through eight-power binoculars when a disc or ball-shaped object appeared in the sky. It was about the size of a full moon, and, after hovering for 15 to 20 seconds, it turned from white to red and began drifting away. As the disc began to move, a shining, cobweb-like substance poured out of it and floated down to earth.

The long, silvery webbing draped itself on trees, telephone poles and lawns like a fluffy blanket, almost ephemeral in its spun glass delicacy.

School children arrived on bicycles and attempted to scoop up handfuls, but the strands simply vanished in their fingers. A photographer from the local *Valley Times* newspaper showed up in time to capture the strands on film, but no other evidence of the mysterious strands lasted long enough to be studied.

The dissipation of collected samples has always thwarted scientific examination of angel's hair. After a 1958 cobweb storm in Trinidad, California, residents tried to collect strands in a glass jar but the substance dissipated before it could be taken to a lab.

According to William R. Corliss, author of *Handbook of Unusual Natural Phenomena,* "Naturalists have long recognized that some species of spiders migrate by casting a strand of cobweb into a breeze and hanging on while the wind carried it aloft. On occasion, floating cobwebs may descend in incredible quantities but, curiously, there is no mention in any of the reports of the presence of spiders in this general shower of webs.

"Under some conditions, the single strand of cobweb agglomerate to form wads and raglike patches of white material. With bright sunlight reflecting on these masses, one might suspect a flight of UFOs. Threadlike material termed 'angel hair' has long been associated with UFO sightings; it is easy to imagine these reports of 'flying saucers' spewing out webbing have not been exaggerated."

The role of "angel hair" as part of the general UFO riddle remains unclear; it may be that the webbing itself is mistaken for UFOs, or that the webbing is produced by UFOs.

Obtaining physical evidence to prove or disprove the existence of UFOs has always been exasperatingly difficult. Flying saucers invariably come and go without leaving a trace. They have, however, occasionally been photographed. UFO photos were always eagerly sought by the Giant Rock Convention attendees. A singularly remarkable photo was widely examined by the UFOlogists at the 1967 convention. It was a picture of an alien craft unlike any previous photos.

The snapshot was taken by a Yorba Linda teenager who later asked to be called only "Tom." Prior to his sighting, Tom cared little about the subject of UFOs; like many boys his age, his primary interests were basketball and girls. He said that one night a UFO showed up outside his bedroom window and hovered.

In spite of his alarm, Tom reacted quickly. He dug out his camera —a cheap, little Mark XII fixed-focus model— and snapped a single picture. The UFO had flown some distance away by this time but it was still clearly in view.

Tom decided not to trust his film to drug store processing. Instead he took it to a teenage friend to develop. Unfortunately, the single exposure came back under-exposed and fogged. Nevertheless, the object's dramatic silhouette stood out blunt and clear and improbable.

The object was shaped like a brimless hat with four leg-like arms extending out from the rim as if they were landing gears. It was either completely black or very dark red. If the power poles which appear in the foreground serve for size comparison, it was large but not huge.

When Tom's photograph appeared in the local newspaper, it attracted widespread attention. The National Investigations Committee on Aerial Phenomena (NICAP) examined the photograph and declared it to be a clever fake, a small model suspended at the window and photographed by a closeup lens. Then, after professional cleaning and enhancement was done and densitometer readings were made, the photo was judged genuine by a major California aerospace firm. The film showed a grainy image of an airborne metallic object flying across the sky.

But what kind of object was it? Was it piloted or remotely controlled? And why was it peeking in Tom's bedroom?

Proving the UFO photos are real and not hoaxes has always been exasperatingly difficult. But eye-witness accounts without photos are even more unsubstantiable. The strongest cases are always those with multiple witnesses. If enough reliable people come forward to report an unexplained sighting, their reports are much harder to dismiss than one from a single person who suddenly confronts something utterly unbelievable.

One of the biggest mass-sightings in the annals of UFOlogy took place in Redlands, California on a quiet Sunday evening in February, 1968. There wasn't much going on that night in Redland, but quite a few people were on the streets or in their back yards. The congregation of the local Methodist Church was arriving for the 7:30 services.

Suddenly, seemingly out of nowhere, a large flying saucer appeared high in the sky above Columbus Street. It was estimated to be about 30 feet in diameter traveling northeast at approximately 300 feet above the earth. The object drifted to a stop and hovered briefly before shooting forward to halt and hover again. Then, as more than 200 people watched, it flew straight up and out of sight. Within a day or two, the Aerial Phenomena Research Organization (APRO) arranged to have four University of Redlands' professors conduct an investigation of the sighting. The team consisted of a geologist, a mathematician, a chemist, and an artist.

Together, they learned that no regular aircraft was scheduled to be over Redlands at that time. The object was not picked up by radar, probably due to the mountain range between the town and March Air Force Base near Riverside. As far as they could determine, the object could not be attributed to any known natural phenomenon.

The artist, John Brownfield, made several detailed colored sketches based on eyewitness descriptions. A composite drawing of the UFO showed it to be a classic saucer shape resembling an enormous Frisbee with a row of seven lighted portholes around the rim.

Brownfield's pictures were a big hit at the 16th annual Giant Rock Space Convention. By now, however, the era of the great flying saucer conventions was drawing to a close; the last one was held in the spring of 1970. George Van Tassel had become elderly and lacked the energy to continue to host the annual conventions. Many of the original contactees were also growing too old, and several had passed on. One in particular was missed more than any other. That man was George Adamski, and his stories are told in the next chapter.

Bibliography - Chapter 11

Corliss, William R. **Handbook of Unusual Natural Phenomena**. New York. Arlington House. 1987.

Paulson, Larry. *Valley Times* newspaper. Puente, California. February 2, 1954.

Randle, Kevin D. **The UFO Casebook**. New York, Warner Books. 1989.

The San Francisco Call. Oakland Office. November 23, 1896.

Spencer, John. **World Atlas of UFOs**. New York. Smithmark Publishers, Inc. 1992.

Story, Ronald D. **The Encyclopedia of UFOs**. New York. Dolphin Books. 1980.

12

George Adamski and his Space Brother

George Adamski, who died in 1965, was perhaps the dean of all those who claimed to have been contacted by beings in outer space and taken into their confidence. His stories, which he told and retold countless times, were so incredible that surely no one would have believed them at all had it not been for his photographs. Over a period of eight years, from 1946 to 1953, Adamski took more flying saucer photographs than anyone else on earth. Even now, more than four decades later, UFOlogists continue to puzzle over these pictures while debunkers still try to prove them hoaxes.

George Adamski was a skywatcher. As a retired school teacher, he had many hobbies, but he particularly enjoyed astronomy. He was never happier than when he stood beneath a star-filled sky with his eye pressed to the eyepiece of his small, portable telescope. Adamski always marveled at the immensity of the universe, its incomprehensibility, and his own insignificance by comparison.

Adamski's home was ideally situated for sky-watching. He lived in Palomar Gardens, a mere 11 miles from the great, white-domed observatory where the huge 200-inch Hale telescope is housed. His own little telescope had been given to him in the late 1930s by one of his students. Mounted on a tripod, it could be easily set up wherever Adamski desired. A camera could be attached over the eyepiece, allowing him to make observations and shoot pictures simultaneously.

Until 1946, George Adamski recorded only known celestial objects; he never saw nor photographed anything that shouldn't be out in the awesome panorama of stars on display silently above him.

Then, on the ninth of November, Adamski gathered with some of his neighbors in his backyard and spent over two delightful hours watching a brilliant rain of falling stars. Just as the most intense part of the shower was ending, someone called out "Look! A space ship!"

A long, cigar-shaped object had become visible in the sky high over the mountain ridge south of Mount Palomar. As he watched, the motionless object abruptly pointed its nose up and shot off into space, leaving behind a long, fiery, red trail which lingered in the sky before fading away.

Adamski refused to believe it was a space ship. He assumed it was some sort of new military aircraft developed during the war. But, less than a week later, he was sitting by himself in his yard swing, from which he could watch the night sky in any direction. As he rocked slowly back and forth, a round, white light shot across the sky going from east to west over the southern ridgeline. Adamski was on his feet in an instant. As he stared in disbelief, a second light followed the first. Then another, and another. Soon 32 individual lights had flown over the horizon.

That night changed Adamski forever. From that night on, George Adamski spent every possible moment outdoors looking for UFOs. He expanded his viewing range from his backyard to the outskirts of the wild, undeveloped country beyond Mount Palomar. Though he never again saw an array of lights as grandiose as those of November 9, 1946, his vigilance was rewarded with occasional sightings of bright, aerial objects moving swiftly and purposefully through Earth's atmosphere.

Adamski's early attempts at photographing these aberrations were largely unsuccessful; the fast-moving objects came out blurred and fuzzy on film. Still, now and then, he captured some remarkable images of shining, circular lights and tilted discs. Soon, his best photos began appearing in the *San Diego Journal*, the *San Diego Tribune-Sun*, and *Fate Magazine*.

Adamski followed a strict procedure in the development of his film. After he shot the picture, he took it in its original holder to a professional photographer, D.J. Detwiller of Carlsbad, for developing. No other hands touched the film before the final prints were made; the possibility of film tampering after the film was exposed was nil.

During 1952, the old skywatcher began taking trips into the desert a considerable distance from Palomar Gardens to places well away from maintained roads and highways. Here, in these remote, desolate places, he made some incredible sightings— both by day and by night. He could not explain how he picked these places: he said he simply had a feeling he was supposed to go there.

On November 20, 1952, he took a group of his friends to one of those lonely places not far from Blythe. The sky was clear and blue as the small group drove out into the desert. The terrain was rough and rocky; clumps of silver-grey desert holly with blood-red berries grew amid the sharp, dark volcanic boulders.

All morning, they watched the wide, empty sky in vain. At noon, they opened their picnic basket and ate sandwiches. Suddenly, Adamski dropped the hard-boiled egg he was peeling and let out a cry.

High above the hills, an enormous, long, black object had appeared and was cruising silently across the bright sky. Adamski grabbed his camera and jumped into the passenger side of his new car. "Lucy," he said to one of his companions, "You drive. Let's follow that thing as far as we can."

The car roared onto the dusty, rock-studded rut road, but before the pair had driven a full mile, the mysterious spaceship drifted over the nearby hills and out of sight.

"Stop the car, Lucy," George requested. "I'm getting out. I think this is where I'm supposed to be. And," he added enigmatically, "I think I'm supposed to be alone."

Puzzled but hopeful that the old man knew what he was doing, Lucy drove back to the others. Within moments, a shiny, silver flying disc came into view, moving at a moderate speed and following the flight path of the larger ship. Hastily, he raised his camera and began taking pictures. Adamski's camera, like his telescope, was nearly an antique, and old Hagee-Dresden Grafles.

A CLASSIC GEORGE ADAMSKI PHOTO. Without photos like this one, no one would have believed his tale of brotherhood with a visitor from outer space.

The British Book Center

Squinting hard, he soon realized a lone man was walking down the rocky slope and heading directly toward him. The two men approached, halted, and stood talking for over an hour. Then, almost as if at a signal, a magnificent flying saucer rose from behind a ridge. The beautiful bell-shaped ship radiated the sun's rays like a smoky diamond as it moved forward until it reached the two figures and hovered beside them. Apparently, the strange man then boarded the craft, for he was gone when it flew away.

Standing alone now, Adamski waved his hat happily in the air. His friends wasted no time driving down to join him. The old fellow was incoherent and ecstatic as he described his experiences. Both the man and the ship were from Venus, he claimed. The space traveler was quite human in appearance except for his shoulder length hair, unusual for a male in 1952. He had communicated with Adamski through a combination of hand gestures and mental telepathy, and his message was both reassuring and disturbing.

"He said they're monitoring what we're doing to ourselves and our world," Adamski explained. "They're worried about us." But the spaceman had gone on to emphasize that not all extraterrestrials visiting Earth come from this solar system. Many are from far distant galaxies, he said. Some are extremely strange creatures, very different from human beings. And not all are friendly.

"Just before he left, I asked if I could take his picture, and he said no," Adamski lamented. "However, I did manage to snap a shot of his ship as it lifted off. I sure hope it turns out."

Adamski needn't have worried. The hastily taken photo proved to be the most sensational UFO picture of its time. Encouraged by many UFO believers' acceptance of his photo, Adamski continued his skywatching. Soon he was reporting additional contacts with his "space brother" and he confided to a few close friends —including P.J. Detwiller— that he expected to be traveling into outer space soon himself.

One day in early 1953, Adamski told his friends he had an irresistible urge to go to Los Angeles. The next morning, he boarded a bus and rode into the city. Twenty-four hours later, he was back with an incredible story to tell.

From the bus depot, he walked to a nearby hotel and checked in. It was late afternoon, so Adamski passed some time in a cocktail lounge. Later, he had a leisurely supper in the dining room. Afterwards, he bought a newspaper and sat in the hotel lobby facing the door. And there he waited.

The time went by slowly. When ten o'clock came, Adamski was beginning to believe he made a mistake. Then, as he was about to go up to his room, two strangers entered the lobby. They glanced about, spotted Adamski and walked directly to him.

George Adamski eyed the strangers closely. There was nothing out of the ordinary about them. They wore plain business suits, narrow ties, and snap-brim hats. They were clean-shaven and their hair was short in the fashion of the day.

Adamski rose from his chair as the men extended their hands to him. When he put out his own hand, each of the two men simply pressed their palms lightly across Adamski's palm. The old man smiled happily. "So you have come," he beamed. "I knew you would!"

"We are sorry we couldn't have picked you up sooner, Mr. Adamski," said the taller of the two men.

"But we are taking you to someplace where it is best if we are there late at night. Are you ready to go?"

Without hesitation, Adamski followed the two men trustingly into the street. They all climbed in a late model Pontiac sedan and drove off into the Los Angeles night. As they drove along, the men explained a little about themselves. They were from Mars and Saturn respectively and had been living and working among Earth people for several years. In Los Angeles, they blended in so well that no one suspected they were carefully studying humans first hand.

Through mental telepathy, they and their comrades in the space ships had monitored George Adamski's thoughts. They had unanimously agreed he was worthy of becoming one of the specially selected few with whom contact should be made. Now, he was being taken to meet others so he could see the space ships for himself.

Adamski was thrilled, to say the least. He rode in silence as the car left the city and headed into the open space beyond. For 15 minutes, they traveled on a rough, narrow dirt road. Finally Adamski saw a soft, white glowing object sitting on the ground in the distance.

The Martian parked the car within 50 feet of the saucer and Adamski noticed at once that it was identical to the one he had photographed three months earlier. His Venusian space brother brother was standing beside the ship, smiling.

After they pressed their hands together, Adamski was taken on board. The interior consisted of a single circular room the diameter of which he estimated to be about 18 feet. Two foot-thick pillars extended from the top of the dome to the center of the floor. This, Adamski was told, was a magnetic pole which drew on "nature's forces" for propulsion.

Two small but comfortable benches curved around the cabin and, after Adamski had seated himself, the Venusian sat down at the control panel and began pushing buttons. Adamski felt only a slight sense of movement as the saucer left the ground, but, within seconds, he was looking down through a huge lens around the base of the pillar at the lights of Earth far below.

Only a few minutes passed before the Saturnian said, "Be prepared for landing. We are nearing our mother ship."

Adamski peered out of the porthole. Across from him, a gigantic black shadow hung motionless in the stratosphere. As the scout ship slowly drew closer, the great, cigar-shaped carrier seemed to stretch away almost out of sight. "She is nearly 2,000 feet in length," the Martian explained. "150 feet in diameter."

As the saucer glided down toward the mother ship, a curved hatch opened up on the far end of the cylindrical body and the little craft drifted inside. The craft touched down on a pair of shiny rails and rolled smoothly into a large storage hangar where several other scout ships sat poised in a row.

The door of the saucer opened up and all four men stepped out into the great majestic ship. Adamski followed his companions into the control room. The walls were covered with colored graphs and electronic charts, and many complex instruments and a powerful telescope could be seen on a large platform 40 feet above the floor.

From here, the group entered the ship's lounge, or "living room," as Adamski called it. The room was suffused in a soft, blue-white light and its tables and chairs beckoned to him. Two golden-eyed young women rose to greet them. They were both dressed in brown flight suits with orange trim on their waistbands and shoulder patches on their sleeves depicting a planet encircled by a ring. "Saturnians," Adamski thought "They seem so young to be pilots."

In answer to Adamski's unspoken thoughts, the Saturnian male said. "Appearances can be deceiving, my friend. Though they look to be in their twenties, Kalna and Ilmuth are between 200 and 300 years of age. Soon, you will meet the one we call "The Master." He is over a thousand years old in his present body and is wiser than all the rest of us.'

The small group seated themselves around a table and Adamski was offered a crystal goblet of fruit juice. As they sipped and talked, a door opened and an elderly man entered the lounge. He wore a brown pilot's tunic and his face was wrinkled with age. After greeting Adamski with a press of his hand, he joined the others at the table.

To Adamski, he said, "My son, you have been brought here so you will see the reality of our space crafts. And, so you can look at a tiny part of the universe from 50,000 miles above your own small planet.

"You will notice we have no weapons of destruction aboard our ships. Our mission is a peaceful one. If we are attacked, the electromagnetic radiations from the ships will protect us. But, if the situation arises when it is merely our lives against the lives of our brothers and sisters —even the belligerent ones of your planet Earth— we would allow ourselves to be destroyed rather than to slay a single fellow being.

"Of all the planets in this solar system, only on your world does brother fight brother. Only on Earth are weapons of assured mutual suicide produced. In all of our colonies on Mars, Venus, and Saturn, life is serene. All of our technology is applied to the betterment of life."

For the next hour, George Adamski listened as The Master told of the space traveler's mission to Earth, of how they constantly observe and monitor the activities of humanity. The old alien expressed great concern over the development of the atomic bomb and its use in war and reckless testing. Until the people of Earth learned to live in peace and harmony with one another, the saucers dared not land and share their highly advanced technology, for it would be devastatingly misused.

Contact could be made only with a limited number of carefully selected individuals whose duty it would be to spread the extraterrestrials' message as widely as possible. George Adamski was one of the chosen few.

"It is time for you to return to your home," said The Master. "But you will be brought back again to experience greater wonders than you have seen tonight."

Reluctantly, Adamski reboarded the scout ship and was taken back to Earth. Less than two hours after landing, he was standing in front of his hotel saying goodbye to his new friends. Though Adamski had been up all night, he was wide awake. He spent a restless hour lying on his bed reliving his experiences of the previous night. Then, shortly after dawn, he caught a bus back to Palmar Gardens.

Now, time crawled by more slowly than ever as Adamski awaited his next contact. But, within a few days, he awoke one April morning with the same overpowering desire to visit Los Angeles. This time, Adamski had no qualms about going. By evening, he was sitting in the lobby of the same hotel anticipating the arrival of his alien friends in suits. At ten on the dot, they both walked through the door.

The drive to the landing site went quickly. Upon arrival, Adamski noticed that the waiting saucer was much bigger than the previous scout craft, nearly 150 feet in diameter. "This is our larger type of scout," the Saturnian explained. "It is designed for long range travel and can remain away from its mother ship for a week or more without recharging."

Adamski's heart skipped a beat. Long range travel? Could he dare to hope he was to be taken to outer space?

Reading his mind, the Saturnian smiled. "Yes, we have been given permission to take you on a little trip tonight. How would you like to visit the moon, Mr. Adamski?"

George Adamski's knees sagged, and, in trembling awestruck amazement, he nodded his head. Dazed, he allowed himself to be escorted on board. Once he was seated within the central chamber, the door closed and the vehicle hummed as it rose from the ground and flashed away into the blackness.

By looking through one of the portholes, Adamski could see the full moon growing larger and larger until it filled his peripheral vision. Close up, it looked like a great earthly desert; its deep valleys and craters were white, barren, shadowy, and pristine.

The Martian joined Adamski at the porthole. "This side of your moon is hot and dry," he said. "But the other side —the dark side your people have never seen— is more temperate. It is there we have constructed a permanent base which you will soon see."

The spacecraft sailed grandly over the moon's rim and curved around into darkness. Before long, Adamski spied a small, distant cluster of lights in the perpetual night. As the spaceship drew nearer, the old man realized that they were approaching a miniature city in the middle of an otherwise empty landscape.

The ship halted and hovered above the moon base and Adamski went at once to the giant telescopic lens in the center of the craft's floor. He found himself looking down at the magnified images of the roofs of tall buildings. The buildings rose along well-lit streets upon which big, bus-like vehicles were moving. Large landing pads, hangars, and storage facilities stood on the outskirts of the town. It all glittered like a city that never slept.

"Unfortunately, we cannot land," said the Martian. "Even with our advanced technology, it takes over a week to adjust to the rarified atmosphere and gravitational peculiarities of the moon. You cannot leave the ship, Mr. Adamski. But trust your eyes and know that everything you see is real."

"But how can you live in such an inhospitable place?" Adamski wondered.

"Think of your own Antarctica," the Martian replied. "A man cannot survive there unprotected but in the bases you have built, he can live quite comfortably. And think of your submarines within which men can live beneath the surface of the sea. Anything is possible if science is advanced enough."

Adamski stared at the lunar miracle, amazed. Then, all too soon, the saucer shot straight up and flew away to head for the open foothills outside the very different city of Los Angeles.

In the days that followed Adamski's second space ride, the old man began to get worried. He wanted very much to tell his fellow earthlings about his marvelous experiences, but who would believe him? He had flown in flying saucers, been on board a moth-

ership and visited the dark side of the moon. And he
had new alien friends who were hundreds of year
older than he. If he told his stories, as he fully intended to do, who would listen? Who would think he was
anything other than a self-deluded, senile old fool?

Adamski had no proof to substantiate his wild
claims. Therefore, on the evening of Adamski's third
hotel rendezvous, his alien friends found him seated
in the hotel lobby with his trusty old Hagee-Dresden
Grafles perched in his lap.

He asked —indeed, he implored— his contacts
to allow him to take pictures aboard the spaceships.
The space men readily granted permission and George
Adamski, clutching his camera with his pockets
stuffed with film holders, rode to the landing site.

Once they were in flight, he attempted to photograph the scout's interior but the light was dim and
his meter readings were poor. Disappointed, Adamski
sat dejected on a curved bench. Then, at approximately one-half mile from the floating mother ship, the
craft came to a halt and hovered. "We will have to wait
a few minutes before landing, Mr. Adamski," the Saturnian said. "A flight of scout ships is about to leave
the carrier. Perhaps this will present an opportunity
for you to take some more pictures."

Adamski hurried to a porthole. Outside, he
could clearly see the giant mothership hanging darkly
in the empty sky. The hatch on the top was open, and,
as he watched, a glowing, disc shaped object floated
out. Adamski clicked his shutter.

The shining disc paused near the mothership
while a second luminous scout emerged. Adamski
snapped another picture. Before long, six scouts had
come out and Adamski got six pictures. He returned
to his seat feeling much better.

Now, the Venusian scout moved smoothly into the carrier ship and Adamski was taken again to the lounge where he saw a feast had been laid out on a long table. The banquet, he was told, was to celebrate the departure of his Martian and Saturnian friends. Their missions on Earth were completed and they were returning to their home planets.

Adamski accepted this news with both happiness and sorrow. He was glad his friends were going home but was saddened by the realization that he would never see them again. In fact, a disturbing thought arose in his mind. He was beginning to feel sure that this was his last ride into outer space. Without his earthly contacts, he would lose touch with his brothers and sisters except through telepathy.

"Well," Adamski thought. "If this is to be our last night together, what better way to spend it than at a farewell banquet?"

The feast, as Adamski expected, was vegetarian. Delicious fruits and vegetables were served along with a dark, porous bread. A single slice of the bread, he was told, contained twice the protein of a pound of meat.

After the meal, beautiful music came out of the walls and filled the room. Adamski's earthly contacts changed from business suits to robes, and joined two women in a lively dance. The dance was performed to express their joy at returning to their homes. Adamski was deeply moved. It was a perfect farewell.

As soon as Adamski was back in California, he went at once to D.J. Detwiller's studio in Carlsbad to turn in his film. As always, his face bore a broad smile. "George," he said. "I don't know where in hell you took these pictures, but they're fantastic!"

The pictures Adamski shot in the interior of the

saucer did not turn out. They were completely under-exposed, as he was sure they would be. But the others, the six of the mothership and the emerging scouts, were sensational.

The glow of the saucers lit up the dark body of the huge spacecraft as it loomed in the night sky, creating a scene as otherworldly as any Earthbound mortal could imagine. George Adamski's sigh of relief was almost a cry of exultation.

Now, he had proof of his journeys. Now, he could use his photos to illustrate the books he planned to write, and he could display them at the lectures he planned to give. True, they would be challenged by experts and scoffed at by skeptics, but they could not be rejected as fakes or accidents in the development process. The images, whatever they were of, were real and not to be dismissed or ignored.

During the coming months, George Adamski wrote two successful books and delivered countless lectures to bring his message from the stars to as many people as would listen. He did not succeed in changing the destructive direction of humanity but he added his distinctive, lonely voice to those many others speaking out about the same topics. Adamski was articulate, impassioned and sincere. No doubt, his friends in outer space were very proud of him.

To this day, the scores of pictures he took over a period of eight years are still being reprinted and argued over. To some, he was the dean of all contactees; to others, just a mischievous old fraud.

George Adamski always said that he was undisturbed by the many attempts to discredit him. "Every man is free to believe or disbelieve that space has been conquered by people from planets far advanced beyond our own," he wrote once. "One's personal conclusions in no way alter this reality. The Earthbound mind must face the fact that miracles and new wonders await discovery in the unlimited Universe in which we dwell."

Even his severest critics had to agree with him on that.

Bibliography - Chapter 12

Adamski, George. **Inside the Space Ships**. New York. Abelard-Schuman, Inc. 1953.

Corliss, William R. **Handbook of Unusual Natural Phenomena**. New York. Arlington House. 1987.

Leslie, Desmond and Adamski, George. **Flying Saucers Have Landed**. New York. The British Book Centre. 1953.

Randle, Kevin D. **The UFO Casebook**. New York. Warner Books. 1989.

Spencer, John. **World Atlas of UFOs**. New York. Smithmark Publishers Inc. 1992.

Story, Ronald D. **The Encyclopedia of UFOs**. New York. Dolphin Books. 1980.

13

Knockin' on Heaven's Gate

Not all those who possess a faith in their own immortality choose to wait passively for their current lives to pass and the next, or higher, stage to begin. Some true believers not only have lost their fear of death, but embrace it as a tool of spiritual transition.

Such was the decision of the 39 members of a once obscure and minor cult known simply as Heaven's Gate.

In late March of 1997, this small group of gentle souls shocked the world by blissfully and serenely shedding their "earthly containers" in the largest mass suicide in the United States, perhaps excepting the fiery deaths at Waco. They died not in an anguished state of crazed paranoia but in a joyous, exalted mood.

The Heaven's Gate cultists had waited a long time to receive the signal that would tell them to "walk out the door of their lives" and go on an intergalactic voyage to a higher place. Every night, this self-proclaimed "Next Level Crew" would watch the skies above their lavish rented mansion in the luxurious, secluded bedroom community of Rancho Santa Fe north of San Diego. Finally, a celestial "marker" appeared above them in the form of the majestic comet Hale-Bopp.

To the cultists, there could be little doubt that this was their long-anticipated sign. And when they learned from the Internet and Art Bell's syndicated talk show that an enormous UFO was supposedly following in the comet's slipstream, they were sure it was time. The often-predicted spacecraft was clearly coming at last from the Level Above Human to take them all home to Their World. Preparation for the cosmic rendezvous began.

Everyone realized they would have to leave their bodies behind. This was really no problem, for, as they all knew, the human body is but a "vehicle" for the soul, a hindrance to spiritual development. However, getting other people —those who were still unenlightened— to understand this would be difficult. Therefore, the first order of business had to be the videotaping of exit statements.

These farewell tapes are surely some of the eeriest home movies ever made. Smiling in the bright California sunshine, the doomed disciples posed beneath the trees in the mansion's breezy back yard and light-heartedly discussed their impending deaths.

"We couldn't be happier about what we're about to do," declared a middle-aged man. "I couldn't have made a better choice," laughed a young woman. "We're really looking forward to this," agreed another. "Beam me up!" chuckled someone else.

Once the goodbyes had all been said, it was time for everyone to have a bit of fun and enjoy their last few days as humans. As always, the whole cult went out as a group, dressed identically in baggy black pajamas. They went out for pizza and a movie.

The following night they all ate out again, this time at the upscale Red Oak Steakhouse. At noon the next day, they paid a last visit to their favorite restaurant, Marie Callender's in Carlsbad. Each member chose a chicken pot pie and had cheesecake for dessert. That night, March 21, Hale-Bopp burned its brightest as it arced nearest to Earth. The time had come.

Heaven's Gate members died in groups. The first 15 exited their vehicles on Saturday March 22 in a neat and tidy fashion, departing as quietly and calmly as they had lived. Following written instructions, they carefully packed overnight bags with clothing, spiral notebooks, and lip balm. In the pockets of their baggy black trousers, each one carried a five-dollar bill, a roll of quarters, and full identification, while on the left sleeve of their loose black shirts, an arm patch reading "Heaven's Gate Away Team" had been sewn.

Each wore a brand-new pair of black and white Nike running shoes and those who wore glasses folded them and set them aside. After consuming little cups of phenobarbital-laced applesauce, and chasing it down with a shot of vodka, they allowed plastic bags to be placed over their heads and secured around their necks with elastic bands. Then, they followed the last instruction: to "lay back and relax" beneath diamond-shaped purple shrouds on individual bunk beds, waiting for their ascension to the Next Level.

Another 15 departed in the same manner the next day, and the remaining cultists killed themselves on Tuesday, March 25. All seven bedrooms were now filled with corpses, lying side by side in rows, together in death as they had been in life. Only the Heaven's Gate's leader died alone.

In the great master bedroom at the end of a long second floor hallway, the cult's guru, a charismatic man who called himself Do (pronounced "doe"), took his life. It was he who had founded this bizarre doomsday movement more than 20 years earlier and it was his strange teachings that had convinced his disciples that they could find salvation through self-destruction.

How had he done it? How had he taken control over so many innocent minds? What kind of man was he? As the answers to these questions emerged during the aftermath of the tragedy, a disturbing portrait formed.

The guru's real name was Marshall Herff Applewhite, born in 1931 to a wandering Texas preacher. His early life seems to have been fairly ordinary. After college, he pursued a career as a music teacher to support his wife and two children. Those who knew him during those days agree he was a likeable fellow, both polite and charming. No one knew that beneath the surface he was a deeply troubled man.

By the age of 30, Applewhite had come to the realization that he was gay. In the early 1960s, an

affair he had with a young man destroyed his marriage and cost him his job at the University of Alaba-
ma. Though he found another job teaching at the University of St. Thomas in Houston, he lost it in 1970
due to "health problems of an emotional nature."

He grew more and more unstable, suffered from
depression, began hearing voices and abusing drugs.
In 1971, after a near-death experience from a drug
overdose, he entered a psychiatric hospital, seeking
help. The help he found, however, was not at all what
he expected.

It was there that Applewhite met Bonnie Lu Nettles, an event that changed both of their lives. Nettles,
then 44, was the nurse who attended Applewhite. She
was an astrologer and a channeler of spirits who
claimed to be psychic. She believed at once that the
two of them were linked on a spiritual plane. She told
him that he had a higher purpose in life, just as she
did, and that together, they were destined to find it.
Applewhite agreed, and from that time on they were
inseparable companions. "Their relationship wasn't a
romantic thing," Nettles' daughter, Terrie, said years
later. "It was more like a friendship, a platonic thing."

It did not take Nettles and Applewhite long to
convince themselves that they had been infused with
higher heavenly spirits, but it was not until 1973 that
they discovered their true identities. They were probably not terribly surprised when they found themselves
mentioned in the Book of Revelation:

*And I will give power to my witnesses and they
shall prophesy ... And when they have finished their
testimony, the beast that ascendeth out of the bot-
tomless pit shall overcome them and kill them... And
after three days and a half, the spirit of life from God
entered them... and they ascended up to heaven in a*

cloud... and gave glory to God.

Applewhite and Nettles were absolutely sure they were those two witnesses, the successor representatives of Jesus who would appear at the beginning of the End Times and would prepare the way for the Kingdom of Heaven. They would be martyred and would rise up to heaven in a "cloud" —a UFO, obviously. It would be a glorious destiny.

Soon the couple began calling themselves "The Two" and started traveling the country, preaching and seeking followers. Establishing a cult proved to be a slow and difficult task. The would-be prophets had to support themselves doing odd jobs and had numerous brushes with the law. In Harlingen, Texas, they were arrested for stealing gasoline credit cards. Later, Applewhite was charged with auto theft.

Eventually the charges were dropped. Gradually, their fortunes began to rise. Their passionate sermons packed auditoriums; their promises of a flight to salvation aboard a spaceship attracted scores of wide-eyed recruits who willingly gave up their families, sex lives, drugs and money to achieve "Human Individual Metamorphosis."

The Two went through a series of name changes during the cult's early days. Usually, their names were nonsensical in nature. For a while, Applewhite was "Bo" and Nettles "Peep"; then they became "Nincom" and "Poop", "Guinea" and "Pig", and finally the musical notes "Do" and "Ti".

Why did Applewhite and Nettles finally settle on the names "Ti" and "Do?" The answer seems to lie in the esoteric writings of a Russian philosopher early in this century.

The lectures of G.I. Gurdjieff and writings of his disaffected disciple, mathematician Petr Demianovich Ouspensky, author of "The Psychology of Man's Possible Evolution," hold many keys to the Heaven's Gate riddle. Yet in the media frenzy after the cult suicides in 1997, the relevance of these European teachers on Applewhite's world-view was completely overlooked in the race to explain how the tragedy came to pass.

But an Albuquerque, New Mexico, astrologer, Sandy Bryan, and her artist friend, Lee Bowen, were struck by the strong links between what the media reported about Heaven's Gate activities and what they recalled from readings from Gurdjieff and Ouspensky many years earlier.

"My friend is an artist, so she is accustomed to recognizing patterns, shapes and connections that others might miss," said Bryan. "We both remembered several things we had read from the book 'In Search of the Miraculous,' by P.D. Ouspensky, back in the 1970s that so closely resembled what was happening at Heaven's Gate."

She pointed out references to the symbols used in that text and at the California death scene, the significance of the names "Do" and "Ti," and the Gurdjieff insistence on subjugation of individual will, suppression of sexual desires, advancement through levels of human evolution, treatment of the human body as a machine and transcendence over death.

"In Search of the Miraculous: Fragments of an Unknown Teaching," copyrighted in 1949, is filled with symbols, diagrams and equations that seem to have influenced Applewhite and Nettles.

Throughout the book are references, in text and diagrams, of the relationship of the musical scale (do, re, mi, fa, so, la, ti, do) to phases of human evolution. "Ti" and "do," obviously, are the highest levels before changing to the next octave.

Chapter Eleven of Ouspensky's book explores the meaning of Gurdjieff's teaching that "A man may be born, but in order to be born he must first die, and in order to die he must first awake." Another of the Russian philosopher's aphorisms is recorded as "When a man awakes he can die; when he dies he can be born."

Pointing out the similarity of symbols in the book and the arrangement of shrouds that covered Heaven's Gate members corpses, Bryan and Bowen are sure too many coincidences exist between Gurdjieff's teachings and those of Applewhite.

"About 18 years ago, I did a lot of reading about the ideas of Gurdjieff and Ouspensky out of curiosity," said Bowen. "I had half-forgotten all of that until I saw the news coverage about Heaven's Gate, especially the bodies covered with the purple shrouds. When I saw the symbol that the shroud and bodies made I was convinced that the media was overlooking something terribly significant as to how this tragedy happened. I looked at the news photographs, and here was the exact symbolic representation of the diagrams in Gurdjieff's work."

Bowen feels it is important for Americans to realize that "Applewhite did not cook this stuff up all by himself."

"Based on all this, it would seem there was study of the writings of P.D. Ouspensky by members of the cult," Bryan concluded. "The teachings that viewed humans as automatons seems to be echoed by what we know of the Heaven's Gate cult. These writings have been in our culture for some time, but, of course, it would have been pretty esoteric reading."

The Ouspensky book "The Psychology of Man's

Possible Evolution," first published in 1950 in England, includes a description of an advanced human state in which "he is immortal within the limits of the solar system."

As Bryan pored through the two Ouspensky books, she noted, "The more deeply you study this, the more connections you find between these writings and the Heaven's Gate cult."

But if the texts have any reference to a spaceship following a comet they are even more obscure or entirely absent. Still the leaders' subtle insistence on obedience, repression and ritual appealed to some potential followers and repelled others.

The cult's dropout rate was rather high at first since the promised spaceship repeatedly failed to appear. But as the group became better organized, control measures became more stringent. Although no one was forced to obey the rules, and were free to leave any time, the cultists readily accepted the discipline. At their rustic, sequestered camp near Laramie, Wyoming, Do and Ti's disciples lived highly regimented lives. A *Time* magazine reporter who visited the compound in 1979 wrote that the group had literally "thousands of rules." There were procedures for everything. Each busy day began with prayers at three o'clock in the morning and was filled with camp chores, Bible study, and emotion-control classes. Everyone kept hair cropped short and wore loose-fitting jumpsuits to make themselves look neuter and identical. Sex, drugs, and alcohol were strictly forbidden.

Trusting one's own judgment, criticizing a teacher, or offering suggestions was not allowed. No actions could be taken without consulting with a "check partner." Each member was required to take a turn guarding the camp perimeter plus doing shifts as one of the "Rotating Eyes" who monitored the campers' conduct and reported violations.

It was a highly regimented way of life but a necessary part of the preparation for the Conversion Experience. As Applewhite told paranormal writer Brad Steiger, the experience would be "that of the physical, the biological, and chemical changeover from human-level creatures to creatures on the next evolutionary level. Just as a caterpillar has to cease all of its caterpillar activities in order to attain its crystalis, so must the same thing happen to a human who wishes to make the transition.

"The human must say, 'I am going to rise above and overcome all of my human desires and activities and emerge an individual that can enter a realm that is altogether physically different from the human.'"

Steiger was unconvinced. "One could say the two of you are simply offering a romantic kind of escape for someone who may be having financial difficulties, marital problems, or a personality crisis," he said. "Isn't your trip, after all, nothing more than a kind of ultimate denial of the real world with all of it's stresses and a retreat into romantic escapism?"

Applewhite struggled momentarily with Steiger's challenge before saying, "If you're using this trip as a cop-out to escape the unpleasantness in your life, you will not get to the Next Level. There is nothing wrong with becoming tired of your human level of existence and wanting another level of existence, but the motivation has to be because you love your Father in that next level with all that you are."

Clearly, Do and Ti were unwavering in their convictions and quite certain of their final vindication. But they were sensitive to ridicule so they kept a low profile and tried to shun publicity. Then, in 1985, something that was not in The Two's cosmic script occurred. Psychic and astrologer Ti unexpectedly went on to the Higher Level by herself.

The cause of death was liver cancer but the cult members believed her mind was so powerful it had "short circuited her vehicle." Do was bereft and longed to join her as soon as possible, but, in the meanwhile, he stayed in touch with her through "celestial conversations." Ti continued to give advice and was often present at the group's meetings, seated invisibly in a chair placed next to Do's.

During the 1990s, Heaven's Gate changed dramatically with Do's discovery of the Internet. He quickly recognized it as both a new way of attracting recruits and of making a living. The cult not only set up its own Web site, but, on July 4, 1995, it also opened a commercial Web-page design business, Higher Source Contract Enterprises. This novel cult activity proved quite successful and Heaven's Gate became financially secure at last.

At that time, one of the newest and most enthusiastic cult members was a 40 year old Californian named Richard Ford. Like all the others, Ford had joined Heaven's Gate in the hope of "advancing beyond human," but this was not to be his fate. He would play a very different role when the cult's moment of truth finally came.

Heaven's Gate had become nomadic again when Richard Ford joined up so he changed his name to Rio DiAngelo and traveled with the others on their tireless pilgrimage. During 1994, they roamed from California to Maine, "homeless by choice," bonded by faith.

DiAngelo was not allowed to meet Do until the end of his first month of membership. It was explained to him that the Great One did not like the vibrations given off by new members while they struggled to control their anger and tame their lusts. Only when he had "reprogrammed" himself would DiAngelo get to see the mysterious cult leader in person.

And sure enough, one night while everyone was camped out in the desert near Phoenix, Do suddenly stepped out of the darkness and into the firelight. Rio DiAngelo was mesmerized by him immediately and remained a devoted follower for a year and a half.

In the summer of 1995, the wandering cult decided to settle down again. A 40-acre piece of land in the pine covered foothills of New Mexico's Manzano mountains was selected and purchased. Office space was rented in the small nearby town of Mountainair and the locals were soon gawking in wonder as the strangely-dressed band of pale, short-haired "monks" opened up a well-equipped computer business.

Out on the edge of the mountains, the folks in the tiny village of Manzano curiously watched truckload after truckload of used tires and cement sacks rumble by on the dirt road to the property. They noticed that the newcomers never waved back when waved at but seemed polite when stopped at the general store.

Store owner Eddie Castillo remembers a woman who came in to ask if he could drive her to Capillo Peak, a pinnacle visible from the village. She said she had heard that a UFO had crashed there five years earlier and she wanted to see it. Castillo had explained with a smile that there was a Forest Service lookout tower and a popular campground atop the peak but no flying saucer.

Members of the group also obtained permission from another landowner across the Rio Grande in the

Ladrones Mountain area to use a hilltop for a campground classroom. An oval-shaped arrangement of 24
stone seats were arranged in concentric arches facing
two prominent, larger stone seats, presumably to be
occupied by Do and Ti as lecturers.

For nearly eight months, the shy cultists lived
quietly in their 40-acre mountainous compound.
Then, abruptly, they announced they had been "summoned" to California; they put the property up for
sale. A potential buyer, Jim Thorsen, toured the place
and was amazed at what he saw.

The group had been hard at work, felling over 70
ponderosa pines to create a clearing where a giant
structure had been built. Thousands of dirt-filled tires
were stacked for the walls of a maze of rooms and
hallways. Thorsen, a New Mexican militia activist,
could not help but notice the dwelling's fortress-like
appearance; it resembled a bunker meant to be capable of holding off a Waco-type siege.

But whatever Heaven's Gate's original intentions
may have been, they now sold the compound to
Thorsen in April of 1996 and moved away —to Rancho
Santa Fe near San Diego.

By now, Rio DiAngelo was developing mixed
emotions about the cult. While he sincerely wanted to
go to the Next Level, he was not completely sure he
was ready yet. Additionally, the cult's most drastic
rite deeply disturbed him. Several of the male members —including Do— had voluntarily had their testi-
cles surgically removed during trips to Mexico.

The purpose of the castrations was to rid the
men of their sexual longings and to decrease any
innate aggressive urges they might still harbor. They
had also discovered a biblical precedent in Matthew
19:12: "*And there be eunuchs which have made*

*themselves eunuchs for the kingdom of heaven's
sake."*

Rio DiAngelo declined to join the brotherhood of
eunuchs; in many ways the lure of the outside world
still tempted him. In February of 1997, he made up his
mind to leave Heaven's Gate. Rather than just walk
out, he decided to talk directly to Do about it. Strange-
ly enough, the cult leader did not seem upset. He simply asked Di Angelo to give him time for reflection.

Later, he summoned the defecting disciple and
said he had just talked to Ti, that she had given her
approval and urged him to go. Do added mysteriously,
"It's all part of a plan."

Rio DiAngelo became Richard Ford once more
and went to work for a company named InterAct
Entertainment. On Tuesday, March 25, 1997, Ford
received a large FedEx package containing a letter and
two video tapes. Without even viewing the tapes, he
knew what had happened.

The next morning, he told his boss, Nick Mat-
zorkis, "My brothers and sisters are all dead." Together, they drove out to Rancho Santa Fe. Ford went into
the house and came out 20 minutes later, white as a
sheet. "They did it," he said. Shocked, the two men
called police.

Now, Richard knew why Do had encouraged him
to leave Heaven's Gate. He was meant to be a living
witness —an "instrument of clarification"— who
would tell the story of this miraculous religious
accomplishment.

He has tried to do this through interviews and
television appearances. But how can anyone tell the
full story of Heaven's Gate when no one, not even an
insider, knows how to write the epilogue? Who can
answer the final question: Where is the "Heaven's

Gate Away Team" now?

Unless one assumes that death is a dead end street and there is no afterlife, one might believe that the cultist's souls still exist somewhere. Some religious people believe they are burning in Hell for the sin of suicide. Others may believe their souls wander the earth endlessly, pining over their wrongful deaths.

As for Richard Ford himself, he has no doubt that his friends reached that Higher Level they sought. They are outside their bodies now, he believes, and he knows he will join them some day, though not through suicide. "There are," he says, "many roads to Heaven's gate."

Bibliography - Chapter 13

Albuquerque Tribune. Special Reports by Doug Brown, Harrison Fletcher, John Hill, and Jessie Milligan. March 1997.

Elshtain, Jean Bethke. *The New Republic* magazine. Washington, D.C. May 5, 1997.

Newsweek magazine. Special reports by David Daniel, David A. Kaplan, Mark Miller, Evan Thomas, Kenneth Woodward, et.al. New York. Newsweek, Inc. April 7, April 14, 1997.

Ouspensky, P.D. **The Psychology of Man's Possible Evoluton.** Second edition. Vintage Books, Random House, New York, 1974.

Ouspensky, P.D. **In Search of the Miraculous. Fragments of an Unknown Teaching.** Harcourt Brace & Company, New York, 1977.

Skeptical Inquirer. Special reports by Martin Gardner, Paul Kurtz & Joe Nickell. Amherst, New York. The Committee for the Scientific Investigation of Claims of the Paranormal. July/August, 1997.

Steiger, Brad. *UFO Universe*. New York, CGR Publishing Group, Inc. Fall, 1997.

Taylor, John. *Esquire* magazine. New York. Hearst Magazines. June, 1997.

Time magazine. Special reports by Cathy Booth, Howard Chua-Eoan, Elizabeth Gleick, Nancy Harbert, James Willwerth, et al. New York, Time, Inc. August 27, 1979; April 7, April 14, 1997.

.

14

Caves of Mystery, Beauty, and Horror

What is there about caves that beckons so strongly? Why are people who live on the earth's surface drawn so inexorably to explore subterranean depths, to creep, sometimes on hands and knees, into the darkness below the sunshine?

One answer is that caves offer the expectation of wonderment, that something extraordinary must exist below the ground, hidden from the blinking eyes of those who live in the world of daylight. In California, this is certainly true; many of the state's most obscure caves are repositories of mystery. And, in many cases, the caves are galleries of extreme beauty.

In the mountainous Santa Barbara brush country north of the Santa Ynez River, a profusion of caves hide themselves in the dense cover of chaparral, manzanita and chamisa. As caves go, they are less than spectacular; most are small and shallow, and some are mere overhangs. But all are unique in the area, for their interiors have been painted.

This great collection of aboriginal artwork rivals the painted caves of prehistoric Europe. The walls are covered with montages of figures, shapes and designs that are as beautiful as the work of Joan Miro or the murals of Pablo Picasso. And they are as difficult to interpret as any primitive artwork anywhere on earth. Still, California's painted caves are all but unknown and seldom visited.

Until 1960, the extent of these pictograph sites was unknown. At that time, there were 19 recorded locations within the entire area. After two seasons of extensive searching, Campbell Grant found over 65 additional sites. Grant, an associate of the Santa Barbara Museum of Natural History, relied on tips from ranchers, hunters, and forest rangers.

To this day, an equal number probably remain unfound. Sometimes, when a forest fire clears the brush from a hillside, caves are revealed. It is in these caves that rockhounds and off-trail hikers sometimes make astonishing finds. But, for the most part, the caves go unnoticed. The aboriginals obviously knew the land much better than modern people do.

The techniques employed to produce the drawings were surprisingly sophisticated. Occasionally a

CHUMASH CAVE PAINTINGS. Thousands of years before the birth of "Modern Art," California's aboriginal artists were creating these astonishing subterranean murals.

Desert Magazine Archives

series of dots formed the designs, but more frequently bold lines were used. A red star or an intersected circle, for example, could be outlined in black with additional outlines of white and yellow, thus giving a simple design element much more richness.

The pigments, too, were quite advanced in nature. Black was made from either manganese, burned graphite, or charcoal. White pigment was diatomaceous earth. Iron oxide hematite was used to produce reds ranging from dull brick to bright vermillion. Yellow was derived from iron oxide and the subtle greens and blues were serpentine.

These colors were finely ground in stone mortars and mixed with animal fat as a binder. Using portable paint cups of stone, bone, or shell, the pigment was applied with fingers, fiber brushes or pointed sticks. The final effect was stunning and still vibrant, in the protective environment of the cave.

Anthropologists agree that these marvelous murals were created by the Chumash Indians, who controlled the area for several thousand years before the beginning of the Spanish period. The Chumash were a settled people and ocean-going people who built 24-foot canoes to explore the Santa Barbara Channel. They crossed the channel and made it to the islands of Santa Rosa, Santa Cruz and Anacapa, 25 miles away from the mainland.

Little is known of their religious practices, since the Spanish mission system successfully eradicated them. Therefore, the meaning of the cave paintings can only be speculated.

One mistake that all good anthropologists guard against is to assume that because a picture resembles something familiar, it is a depiction of that thing. For example, just because a drawing looks like a fish doesn't necessarily mean it is meant to represent a fish. Contemporary researchers and viewers can only guess at what was in the minds of the ancient artists.

If California's painted caves remain a mysterious, obscure, and hidden away, it is for the best. Vandalism is anthropology's worst enemy and has already destroyed some of these priceless resources. This glorious artwork can best be displayed in its natural setting. The art can therefore only be seen by a fortunate few.

Many of California's most intriguing caves are the most inaccessible, but one in particular seems impossible to relocate. It is commonly referred to as the Lost Iron Door Treasure Cave, and, if it actually does exist as the stories depict it, it is filled with riches beyond belief.

The story of the cave and its wealth has been told and retold around San Diego County for more than a century and a half. It is claimed that shortly before the Mexican-American War, a small group of Spanish padres discovered a little cave somewhere beyond the tiny community of Ramona. The cave was rich in garnets, so the padres, using Indian labor, set up a small gemstone mining operation.

In 1846, when the war between the United States and Mexico ended, a small caravan arrived at the Santa María mission. It was just two ox carts, but both were filled to capacity with nearly all the precious artifacts of the southern missions. Silver bells and candlesticks, jewel-studded communion cups, *retablos*, and statues of the Virgin Mary made the carts groan under the treasures' weight as they fled the occupying American forces.

Behind the two carts a pair of burros dragged a great iron door. The little procession made its way up to the garnet mine, unloaded the cargo into it, and then sealed the cave's entrance with the huge iron door. Then, Indian laborers covered the cave's opening with tons of dirt and rock, successfully concealing the treasure forever from the invading Yankees.

Plenty of rumors spread over the years, of course, but no one could pinpoint the treasure's exact location. Once the people of that generation died off, the last hope of anyone ever finding the lost cave also seemed to have died off.

Then, in 1963, 117 years after the treasure was buried, an old Indian gentleman named Ben Romero confided to an old friend, Donald Morris, that he had always known the approximate location of the mine.

Romero said that his maternal grandmother had, as a child, witnessed the internment of the trove. She had accompanied a group of Indian women who had been sent to provide meals for the workers. When the work was done, the site was carefully marked with a cross chiseled on a flat rock. Carvings were also cut into the trunks of fledgling oak trees.

Ben Romero had often searched for the markers himself but the Santa María Valley was too big. He found nothing. Now, however, he thought it might well be time for a new search. The popularity and effectiveness of metal detectors led him to believe a careful grid-sweep of the valley beyond Ramona could easily locate the buried iron door. If the aged markers could also be located, the site could be quickly and precisely pinned down.

Ben felt he was too old to participate in a new search, but, for a percentage of whatever was found, he would gladly give all the details he could provide. His own searches had led to the discovery of arrowheads and pottery shards in a specific ravine. This area, he believed, was the place to start.

Morris quickly contacted his best friend and prospecting buddy, Justin Sturm. Both men were construction workers with built-up vacation time on their hands. What better way to spend a couple of spare weeks than to go off into the boondocks and make a fortune?

The following weekend, they set forth armed with camping supplies, topographic maps, and a rented metal detector. For several days, their sweeping search yielded no clues. Then, one morning, Sturm came upon a carving on a very old oak tree. The scar on the bark appeared to be a depiction of the bell tower of a Spanish mission, and on the other side of the tree a Christian cross was carved into a rectangle.

All of this seemed to mark the site as sacred ground if not actual church property. Morris and Sturm wondered if the square beneath the cross represented church possessions buried in a chest. They concentrated their search in this immediate area but found nothing more until, at noon on the eleventh day, they sat down to eat lunch in a dry creekbed.

As they munched their sandwiches, they noticed two large stones atop an even bigger rock lying in the gully. The stones did not look like they had been placed there naturally; they appeared to have been stacked.

Hurriedly, the two men crunched through dry leaves to the rocks. They managed to shove the two top rocks aside and beneath, to their delight, they found the chiseled cross on the surface of the boulder. Now, they were absolutely sure they were standing on top of the Lost Iron Door Treasure Cave. Justin Sturm quickly scanned the cross with the metal detector. Immediately the instrument let out a loud screech that sent Justin jumping sideways.

"Damn," Justin swore. "Wouldn't you know this contraption would go on the blink just when we need it most?" However, a check of the detector proved it to be working perfectly. Its headphone and needle were announcing the presence of something very large and metallic beneath the surface of the ground.

Morris and Sturm started digging at once. As the boulder's earthen foundation was composed of rough, chunky decomposed granite, and the temperature was reaching 105 degrees, the excavation went slowly.

Still, within three days, the two men had reached a depth of 24 feet and the metal detector kept urging them to go deeper. Then they hit solid granite.

Believing they were now standing on the roof of the lost cave, they sat down and planned their next move. Their vacation time had run out, along with most of their small budget. Should they go back to San Bernardino, buy dynamite, and arrange for more time off from work? Or should they shelve the project until their financial situation improved and they were better equipped? Were they just yards away from an enormous fortune, or were they a couple of Don Quixotes embarked on a fool's quest?

One thing was certain: they could no longer afford to continue to rent the metal detector. Sturm decided that, before leaving, he would make a final sweep of the entire area to be sure they had not missed anything. He had gone less than a hundred yards from the diggings before he picked up a reading.

The detector was telling him that something fairly small was buried just a few feet beneath him. After quick digging, the duo dug up an aged, hand-forged Spanish mining pick.

This was just the sort of discovery that always turns a casual treasure hunting expedition into an all-consuming crusade. For Sturm and Morris, it was conclusive proof that they were definitely digging in or very close to the right place. They drove directly back to San Bernardino to take out loans, get more time off from work, and stock up on supplies, including plenty of dynamite.

For the next week, they blasted and shoveled their way down to the scary depth of 45 feet below the cross-marked rock. But they still found nothing but more solid rock.

Discouragement set in once again, until, one day, Sturm stumbled across a large piece of pottery not far from the hole. When he pulled it out of the ground, a small, dirt-encrusted object fell out. When he cleaned it off, it proved to be a miniature silver bell, three inches in height and inscribed in Spanish with the words: "In the year of our Lord, 1830."

Sturm and Morris immediately dug up the area around the find but unearthed nothing more than a few pottery shards. Still, if they needed further confirmation of the site's potential, they had it now. Somewhere within this area was a sealed cave stuffed full of antiquities of immeasurable value. The eager treasure seekers were close, but, as Sturm pointed out, "Close only counts in horseshoes."

Morris and Sturm had to give up their quest. They had exhausted their financial resources and could not afford to take more time off. Although they vowed, as all treasure hunters do, to return someday, they never did. The Lost Iron Door Treasure Cave still waits to be found.

Sometimes, the rediscovery of a forgotten cavern can lead to startling, even horrifying, findings.

Such is the case of a deep and dangerous shaft-like cave in the Big Sur country not far from the little cliff-side community of Lucía. Here, along the spectacularly beautiful coastline, Cape San Martín juts out to defy the ocean. At the tip of the promontory, a rugged, rocky knoll stands defiantly. It was from this stony knob that four San Francisco amateur prospectors saw a dark cloud of bats fly out of the ground one evening in 1962.

Knowing that this surely meant there was a cave among the rocks, the group investigated the next morning. They had no trouble locating the aperture, but the opening proved to be so small they had to do some digging before squeezing inside. Their flashlight beams played over the interior, and, to their shock, they spotted a tangled pile of human bones.

There were seven skeletons total, and all were obviously adults. The four men reported their discovery to the Los Padres National Forest Service. An anthropologist was soon sent out to examine the bones. It was easily determined that all seven had dies of massive head wounds at least a hundred years before. In addition, while six were tentatively identified as Indian, the last was of European descent, probably Spanish.

The reason for the massacre was a much more difficult mystery to solve. Internecine warfare among Indian tribes was quickly ruled out. The Salinan people who inhabited the region at the time had a tradition of cremating or burying their dead. It is quite unlikely they would have dumped bodies unceremoniously in a cave, and it does not explain the presence of the European bones.

One theory sounded promising for a while. According to the legends of the Mission San Antonio, which was located slightly north of Cape San Martín, a small group of Indian converts led by one Spanish soldier set off in the early 1800s to deliver a sizeable fortune in gold coins to a Spanish galleon anchored in Willow Creek Harbor. The tiny expedition disappeared without a trace along with all of the gold, valued at $50,000.

It was believed the small detachment had been ambushed by bandits, possibly mutineers from the galleon itself. If so, it was a perfect heist and seven unsolved murders were committed. At first glance, this theory is enticing. Examined more closely, however, it does not quite fit.

The Forest Service's anthropologist verified the skeletal remains to be approximately 100 years old, not 150. Furthermore, the mission was a poor one, and unlikely to have $50,000 in gold on hand. Proponents claim that the money came from the sale of horses but archival records give no mention of such a sizeable transaction.

Another possibility is that the cave was a gold mine worked by Indian labor under the supervision of Spanish soldiers. When the soldiers were relieved of their duties and sent to a new post, they slew the workers and cast their bodies into the mine to keep its location secret until they could return. If so, the European skeleton remains unexplained.

A third theory has also been advanced. According to this scenario, a group of Indians had discovered the cave and were mining gold within it when a group of non-Indian prospectors showed up. They attacked the Indians, lost one member of their group in the fight, and then disposed of all the bodies.

The main problem with these conjectures is that if the cave was already a mine, it would not have been necessary for the 1962 discoverers to enlarge the opening to crawl inside. That something savage and brutal occurred near the mouth of the cave is undeniable, but what kind of horrifying drama it was will never be known.

The death cave of Cape San Martín may hold its gruesome secrets, but the Moaning Cave of Calaveras County near Vallecitos contains several hundred. If it is difficult to determine the fate of seven bodies in San Martín Cave, it is utterly impossible to uncover the reasons why more than 300 skeletons lie in the depths of Moaning Cavern.

The cave is named for the eerie sounds that emanate from the cavern's mouth. These ghostly noises are caused by air currents, but there are those who swear that the sounds are in fact the voices of the lost souls entombed within the cave.

Moaning Cavern was originally discovered during the Gold Rush. In 1851, a handful of gold seekers entered the cave hoping to find a bonanza. But when they threw their torches down the shaft and watched them vanish into the murky darkness, they decided against further exploration.

Later that same year, California's first state-sponsored geologist, Dr. John Trask, explored the cave quite thoroughly. By rigging ropes and pulleys, he lowered himself and his crew nearly 300 feet into the dank shaft. As he expected, he found no gold, but he did find himself surrounded by a wonderland of stalactites and stalagmites. For the first time in history, his torches illuminated this underground palace filled with Mother Nature's most painstakingly created sculptures.

Trask, to his amazement, also encountered a staggering number of human skeletons. By counting skulls, he estimated there were at least 300. In his report, the geologist wrote, "I will not attempt to speculate on these remains except to say they are presumptive of great antiquity."

The incredible age of the bones is attested to not only by the fact that they are all completely petrified but that many are also actually embedded in the cave's stalactite formations.

Stalactic deposits grow at a maximum rate of 29 years per millimeter or 736 years per inch. In Moaning Cavern, human bone has been found under 16.5 inches of such deposited rock. These particular bones would then be over 12,000 years of age —2,000 years older than Folsom Man.

In 1926, fossil evidence was uncovered proving Folsom Man hunted prehistoric buffalo in New Mexico as early as 8000 B.C. The skeletons of Moaning Cavern show that primitive man was roaming the North American continent even before that time. But why did so many of them wind up in the great cave?

Did they enter the cave seeking shelter only to slip and fall into its terrible depths? Both male and female skeletons were found, so possibly the people went into the cavern in groups rather than as individuals. Perhaps whole families perished.

Or could the cave have been a burial ground, a convenient tomb? Were the bodies simply and unceremoniously tossed in?

Still another, even more chilling theory exists. Could Moaning Cavern have been a place of human sacrifice? Were living people thrown into the pit to appease a wrathful cave god who made unearthly noises before coming forth to stalk the land?

Early man's fascination with caves leaves all these possibilities open to speculation. Caves served our ancestors as shelter during an age when they lacked the ability to build homes. They served as religious shrines where tributes to gods and nature could be painted in abstruse secrecy. And, of course, natural holes in the earth are perfect places to hide both treasures and dark deeds, for there is always an excellent chance they'll never see the light of day again.

In a way, it might be said that most of California's mysteries and miracles are subterranean in this same sense. Lying just below the surface of everyday reality, they usually go unnoticed by unsuspecting passersby. The mysteries that do attract attention often cannot be solved or satisfactorily explained even when closely examined. And those that are solved can quickly be replaced by new, equally perplexing riddles.

Therefore, whenever one travels about the mysterious state of California, it pays to stay alert. Astonishing events can occur at any time in any place. In California, mysteries and miracles are constantly taking place and magic is always afoot.

How to Visit Moaning Cavern

From Sacramento, drive east 43 miles to Placerville. Turn south on Highway 49 for 60 miles to Angels Camp. Just beyond town, turn east on Highway 4 to Vallecito. Moaning Cavern is just south of town. A tour of the cavern is pleasantly adventurous. The first 100 feet is down a metal spiral staircase, and for the more courageous, can be followed by a supervised 180-foot rope rappel, a safe but exciting descent.

Bibliography - Chapter 14

Calirborne, Robert. **The First Americans**. New York. Time-Life Books. 1973.

Grant, Campbell. *Desert* magazine. Palm Desert, California. May, 1964.

Reinstedt, Randall A. *Frontier Times* magazine. Austin, Texas. Western Publication. February/March, 1973.

Sturm, Justin. *Frontier Times* magazine. Austin, Texas. Western Publication. April/May 1964.

Traywick, Ben T. *True Frontier* magazine. Sparta, Illinois. Major Magazines, Inc. December, 1975.